ational Defense Research Institute

Tuition Assistance Usage and First-Term Military Retention

Richard Buddin

Kanika Kapur

RAND

Prepared for the
Office of the Secretary of Defense

The research described in this report was sponsored by the Office of the Secretary of Defense (OSD). The research was conducted in RAND's National Defense Research Institute, a federally funded research and development center supported by the OSD, the Joint Staff, the unified commands, and the defense agencies under Contract DASW01-01-C-0004.

Library of Congress Cataloging-in-Publication Data

Buddin, Richard J., 1951–
    Tuition assistance usage and first-term military retention / Richard Buddin, Kanika Kapur.
      p. cm.
      "MR-1295."
      Includes bibliographical references.
      ISBN 0-8330-3177-5
      1. Student aid—United States. 2. United States—Armed Forces—Pay, allowances, etc. 3. Soldiers—Education, Non-military—United States. 4. United States—Armed Forces—Recruiting, enlistment, etc. 5. United States. Navy—Personnel management. 6. United States. Marine Corps—Personnel management. I. Kapur, Kanika. II. Title.

V698 .B84 2002
355.2'23—dc21

2002069721

RAND is a nonprofit institution that helps improve policy and decisionmaking through research and analysis. RAND® is a registered trademark. RAND's publications do not necessarily reflect the opinions or policies of its research sponsors.

Cover photo courtesy of Fort Leonard Wood at http://www.wood.army.mil

Published 2002 by RAND
1700 Main Street, P.O. Box 2138, Santa Monica, CA 90407-2138
1200 South Hayes Street, Arlington, VA 22202-5050
201 North Craig Street, Suite 202, Pittsburgh, PA 15213-1516
RAND URL: http://www.rand.org/
To order RAND documents or to obtain additional information, contact Distribution Services: Telephone: (310) 451-7002;
Fax: (310) 451-6915; Email: order@rand.org

Tuition assistance (TA) is a military-sponsored program that reimburses military members for the cost of college classes while on active duty. The program is part of a series of quality-of-life efforts designed to make military service more attractive to youth and encourage them to remain in the military. This report examines tuition assistance and retention behavior for first-term members of the Navy and Marine Corps (similar data were not available for other military services). The analysis examines what types of sailors and marines use TA and examines whether TA users are more prone to reenlist than are military members who take no college classes during the first term.

The Deputy Assistant Secretary of Defense for Military Communities and Family Policy sponsored the research. This report should interest those concerned with military families, the well being of service-members, educational opportunities for military members, and the attendant implications of these issues for recruiting and retention.

The research was conducted in the Forces and Resources Policy Center, which is part of RAND's National Defense Research Institute, a federally funded research and development center sponsored by the Office of the Secretary of Defense, the Joint Staff, the unified commands, and the defense agencies.

CONTENTS

FIGURES

TABLES

BACKGROUND

The Department of Defense has long placed a premium on the education of its servicemen and -women. This emphasis is reflected in the efforts to recruit those with high school diplomas and in the support the department provides to those who want to pursue their education once they are on active duty. One of the primary ways the Department of Defense (DoD) supports those on active duty is through the Tuition Assistance (TA) program. Under this program, the military services reimburse their members who enroll in college courses for 75 percent of their tuition expenses up to a maximum of $187.50 per semester hour and $3,500 per individual in any year. Beginning in October 2002, DoD will expand reimbursement under the program to cover 100 percent of tuition expenses up to a maximum of $250 per semester hour and $4,500 per individual in any year. The cost of the program in FY 2000 was just over $157 million.

The program is thought to have a number of benefits. More educated service personnel are seen as being more broadly skilled and thus better at their jobs and with greater potential for advancement than those with less education. Furthermore, the program may enhance the ability of the services to attract youth. More than 60 percent of recruits cite educational opportunities as one of the primary reasons they join the military. Also, some argue that the TA program encourages its participants to reenlist.

PURPOSE AND APPROACH

This research focuses on the effects of TA use on first-term retention. While the TA program serves a variety of purposes, retention is an ongoing concern for the military services, and possible retention effects of TA are the hallmark of TA program reviews. Indeed, Garcia and Joy (1998) have argued that the Navy TA program more than pays for itself in terms of retention benefits alone. This report examines who uses the TA program and whether they are more likely to reenlist than those who take no college courses. Specifically, we focus are first-term enlistees in the Navy and the Marine Corps (similar data was not available for the Army and Air Force).

This report employs two models for the analysis. One is a bivariate probit model of TA usage and retention. This model isolates the direct effect of TA on retention, while adjusting for other factors that affect college enrollment. The second model compares the reenlistment decisions of those who use TA with a similar group of service personnel who did not use the program. This matched sampling or propensity approach has been used in evaluating how civilian job training programs affect subsequent earnings. The two models complement each other and make the overall results more robust.

The report draws from the records of sailors and marines who have completed their first term and are contemplating a second during FY 1997 and the first half of FY 1998. The data file contains information about the member's participation in TA during the two years prior to their reenlistment decision as well as information on his or her demographic characteristics, pay grade, component, and deployments. These latter data are particularly important to the analysis because deployments make it more difficult for service personnel to take college classes. The Navy has responded to ship deployments by establishing the Program for Afloat College Education (PACE), but the fact remains that deployment significantly alters the circumstances for taking college courses. We also gathered qualitative data available on TA from focus group interviews with more than 300 personnel.

RESULTS AND CONCLUSIONS

Who Uses TA?

The overall usage rate for TA during the first term is 8 percent in the Navy and 13 percent in the Marine Corps. Many demographic factors have a similar effect on the participation of sailors and marines.

- Women are much more likely to use TA than are comparable groups of men by about 6 percentage points. Six percent of male sailors use the program, compared with 13 percent of male marines. Among women, 22 percent of sailors use TA, compared with 27 percent of marines.

- Age makes no difference.

- Aptitude makes a difference in the Navy, but not in the Marine Corps.

- Family responsibilities (being married, being a parent, or both) also make a difference for both marines and sailors but only a small one.

- Those with family responsibilities are a few (2 or 3) percentage points less likely to use the program.

Occupation makes a significant difference, even after adjusting for differences in the demographic characteristics of members assigned to those occupations. In both services, those in technical or support and administrative assignments participate in the program more frequently than do those in other types of assignments. This greater participation probably occurs because those working in these occupations have more-predictable work schedules, so it is easier to schedule and participate in college classes. It may also be that those assigned to these types of jobs have more interest in advancing their education.

Assignment also makes a difference. Those assigned overseas are more likely to use TA than are similar personnel who have a domestic assignment. Program use decreases with the number of deployments. Furthermore, sailors assigned to ships are less likely to use the program than comparable groups with shore-based assignments even when those ships are in port and not deployed.[1]

Does TA Affect Reenlistment?

We find that using TA does affect reenlistment—negatively. In the Marine Corps, the typical program participant is about 4 percentage points less likely to reenlist than is a comparable marine who did not participate. In the Navy, the participating sailor is almost 9 percentage points less likely to reenlist than is the sailor who does not participate.

Our results are at odds with those of previous studies (Boesel and Johnson, 1988; Garcia and Joy, 1998; and Garcia et al., 2002) that show TA users are more likely to stay in the military than are nonusers. We show that these studies did not adequately control for the length of time that stayers and leavers were eligible to use TA. Leavers are in the military for substantially less time and inherently less likely to use TA than were similar stayers because they are eligible for fewer months. The authors incorrectly infer that TA users are more likely to stay than nonusers, but the data are simply showing that leavers have more opportunity to use TA. We reestimated these models and showed that TA users were consistently less likely to remain in the military than nonusers, when both groups were eligible for TA for equal periods of time.

The results from our models and reestimation suggest that those who participate in TA do so with an eye to education or work after they leave the service. This is likely to be the case for two reasons. First, a member can accumulate significant college benefits through the GI Bill. Second, the distractions of the work environment, particularly the intense periods of work involved with deployments and the attendant preparation, make it difficult to attend classes regularly. The typical program participant only accumulates six semester hours over two years. At this rate, it would take a long time to accumulate the 60 hours required for an associate's degree or the 120 needed for a bachelor's degree. Thus, those with a strong preference for com-

---

[1]Sailors may take college courses through PACE during sea deployments, but PACE is not analyzed in this report.

pleting a degree may be more likely to go back to civilian society, where they can complete the process much more quickly and with substantial government assistance.

These results do not mean that the program is not worthwhile. Indeed, it may serve as a substantial recruiting incentive, even if an individual joins with no intention of remaining beyond the first term of service. Our focus group sessions indicate that, by and large, servicemembers are enthusiastic about the program, albeit frustrated by the difficulty of meshing classes and work schedules.

ACKNOWLEDGMENTS

We are especially grateful to Gail McGinn, formerly of the Office of the Deputy Assistant Secretary of Defense for Military Communities and Family Policy, for her enthusiasm in initiating this study. Otto Thomas of that office provided valuable advice and information for the research. We are also grateful to Charles Giorlando, at the Navy Campus Management Information System, for providing us with data on TA enrollment.

Among RAND colleagues, we are indebted to Susan Hosek, the former Director of the Forces and Resources Program, and Susan Everingham, the current director of the program, for their support and encouragement. Stephanie Williamson deserves credit for building the complex datasets used in the analysis. We are grateful to Phoenix Do, Sheila Murray, Michael Polich, and Jerry Sollinger for extensive comments on an earlier draft.

AFQT	Armed Forces Qualification Test
ALC	Academic Learning Center
DMDC	Defense Manpower Data Center
DoD	Department of Defense
FY	Fiscal year
GED	General Educational Development (i.e., an alternative school-leaving credential obtained by passing an examination)
IDTC	Interdeployment Training Cycle
MEU	Marine Expeditionary Unit
NCMIS	Navy Campus Management Information System
PACE	Program for Afloat College Education
PERSTEMPO	Personnel Tempo
TA	Tuition Assistance

Chapter One

INTRODUCTION

BACKGROUND

In FY 2000, active-duty military members enrolled in nearly 646,000 college classes under the Tuition Assistance (TA) program. This Department of Defense (DoD) program encourages members to enroll in postsecondary courses while serving in the military. The courses are provided by accredited colleges that agree to offer courses on individual military bases. Military members enroll in a standard university curriculum, and the service branches agree to reimburse the member for 75 percent of tuition expenses up to $187.50 per semester hour. Annual assistance is capped at $3,500 per member per year. The total cost of TA in FY 2000 was $157.3 million dollars.

In special circumstances, the TA program increases aid to 100 percent of tuition costs. The Navy covers all course costs for sailors and marines on ships at sea as part of the Program for Afloat College Education (PACE). This program resulted in 43,000 course enrollments in FY 2000. DoD also requires that the services pay all costs when members are serving in such contingency areas as Bosnia, Kosovo, and Afghanistan.

TA provides off-duty opportunities for members to enhance their general academic skills. The courses reflect a broad range of academic disciplines and are not intended to substitute for direct military job training. College-level instruction may broaden a member's skills and contribute to their success in the military. Indeed, members receive specific promotion point credit for completing college courses.

The military services have provided some form of tuition reimbursement for off-duty education since 1948 (Anderson, 1991). In early congressional testimony, a DoD official explained that the education program was designed so servicemembers could "(1) improve their value to the service; (2) have an opportunity to continue civilian education while in the service; and (3) make profitable use of their spare time" (Anderson, 1991).

In the volunteer force, TA may also enhance the ability of the services to attract young people. Service advertising campaigns herald education opportunities available through the military that include vocational training, college courses while in the service (TA), and educational benefits to cover postmilitary educational expenses. In the 1999 Active-Duty Survey, about 62 percent of military members claim that education benefits and opportunities were a primary reason they joined the military. The survey data do not distinguish between the importance of in-service and postservice education opportunities, but the results show the strong educational interest of incoming members.

PURPOSE OF THIS RESEARCH

This research focuses on the effects of TA usage on first-term retention. While the TA program serves a variety of purposes, retention is an ongoing concern for the military services, and possible retention effects of TA are the hallmark of TA program reviews. Indeed, Garcia and Joy (1998) have argued that the Navy TA program more than pays for itself in terms of retention benefits alone. This research examines what types of members use TA and whether TA users are more prone to reenlist than similar members who do not take college courses. We focus on first-term enlisted members in the Navy and Marine Corps. A similar analysis was planned for the Army and Air Force, but the appropriate data were not available.

If TA has strong positive effects on retention, then it would strengthen the case for enhanced TA efforts. The program has always been multipurpose, however, and the costs may be justified by an expansion of the market for high-quality recruits. The program also has benefits in terms of broadening the academic skills of the military workforce.

This study employs two models for the analysis. One is a bivariate probit model of TA usage and retention. This model isolates the direct effect of TA on retention, while adjusting for other factors that affect college enrollment. The second model compares the reenlistment decisions of those who use TA with a similar group of service personnel who did not use the program. This matched sampling or propensity approach has been used in evaluating how civilian job training programs affect subsequent earnings. The two models complement each other and make the overall results more robust.

DATA

The primary data source consists of two parts. First, month-by-month personnel records provide information on the status of individual sailors and marines throughout their enlistment term. These records include information for each member's demographics, pay grade, pay components, and deployment status as well as a record of the member's reenlistment decision. Second, course enrollment and completion data are recorded for TA participants as part of the course reimbursement procedure. We merged these two data sources to create our analysis database.

In addition to the quantitative data, we also collected qualitative information on TA through a series of base visits as part of a related quality-of-life project (Buddin et. al., 1998; Tiemeyer et. al, 1999). We visited seven bases and met with more than 300 military members as well as education officials at the bases. TA was a popular program among junior enlisted personnel. Nearly all members recognized the importance of continuing their education, whether or not they planned to continue in the military. Many members were frustrated, however, because their schedules did not allow them to take many classes. Work schedules were often unpredictable, so members would miss classes and would fall behind in their studies. In addition, many members have families and struggle to attend classes and meet family responsibilities.

Many young sailors are assigned to ships and have difficulty attending class. They can use PACE while at sea, but ships are frequently undermanned, so work hours are extended during sea duty and study time is limited. Ship crews also have periods of shore time when class attendance is difficult. During a ship's interdeployment training cycle (IDTC), the crew faces a series of inspections and short cruises that make class attendance unpredictable or impossible for long stretches of time. As a result, many sailors are frustrated that they have a narrow window available for attending classes, and it is difficult to accumulate credits.

Young marines have similar frustrations with fitting classroom work into their schedules. Many are part of a Marine Expeditionary Unit (MEU) that has a regularly scheduled six-month deployment at sea. Classes are available though PACE during the deployment, but most members are busy with training and exercises. In addition, each deployment has an intensive six-month work-up period. Field exercises and night training make it difficult for members to attend classes between deployments. In addition, members spend a lot of time away from home, so many spend interdeployment time with their families instead of enrolling in college classes.

STRUCTURE OF THE REPORT

The remainder of the report is divided into four chapters. The next chapter provides our analytic framework and describes our data on TA usage and retention. Chapter Three reports our results for the Marine Corps. Chapter Four documents the findings for the Navy. The final chapter provides conclusions and recommendations.

Chapter Two

ANALYSIS FRAMEWORK AND DATA

A few studies have examined the relationship between TA and retention. However, each of these studies has some aspects likely to skew the results or provide ambiguous results. This chapter reviews several of these studies and identifies the attributes that may distort the results. We begin the chapter by discussing conceptual difficulties in separating the contribution of TA usage to retention. Next, we review the literature on incentives for young adults to attend college, education assistance by civilian employers, and previous studies of military TA. The discussion then turns to the approach used here, which is designed to compensate for the shortcomings of previous studies.

CONCEPTUAL ISSUES

The linkage between TA usage and retention may be complex. A simple comparison of retention for TA users and nonusers might be an inaccurate indication of this linkage, because TA users may be inherently predisposed to stay or leave the military irrespective of their participation in the program. The underlying effect of TA usage on retention can only be disentangled by a careful analysis of the factors that affect both TA usage and retention.

TA usage may affect retention in the Navy or the Marines in several ways. TA usage may improve servicemembers' job performance within the Marines or the Navy and therefore increase promotion opportunities and job satisfaction.[1] On the other hand, TA usage

---

[1] College courses are a requirement for some promotions.

may also increase members' civilian opportunities or spur their interest in leaving the military to become a full-time student. Therefore, a priori, the effect of TA usage on retention is ambiguous and must be empirically determined.

To estimate the effect of TA usage on retention, we must take into account that certain types of individuals are more likely to take TA courses. For example, higher-aptitude or better-educated members may be more likely to use TA. In addition, family situation or military responsibilities may also be tied to TA usage. For example, it might be more difficult for young parents to schedule classes than for single members living in a barracks. Similarly, deployed members may have long work schedules and be unavailable for classes for substantial periods. Each of the factors described in these examples may also directly affect retention. For instance, higher-aptitude individuals may receive better offers from nonmilitary employers or may be more adept at searching for outside offers. As a result, they may be more likely to leave the military. In addition, young parents who may not find the time to take TA courses may also be unlikely to make the time to search for new jobs and, therefore, may be less likely to leave the military.

In the examples above, servicemembers' characteristics are described as directly affecting TA usage and retention. Estimates of the effect of TA usage on retention should not be contaminated by the effect of servicemembers' characteristics (such as aptitude) on TA usage and retention. For example, higher-aptitude servicemembers may be more likely to use TA and may have lower retention; however, this correlation between TA usage and lower retention should not be used to determine the effect of TA usage on retention. TA usage is an endogenous variable affecting retention—i.e., TA usage is determined by direct decisions of the individual and is not predetermined. In contrast, other variables affecting retention, such as gender, aptitude, and deployment status are exogenous variables affecting retention. These variables are predetermined and not subject to the decisions or manipulation of the individual servicemembers that makes the retention decision.

An empirical approach is needed that separates the effects of TA usage from those of other factors affecting retention. Recent studies have begun to handle this problem, and our approach attempts to improve on these methods.

LITERATURE REVIEW

Several studies of young adults have shown substantial economic returns to college attendance even if that attendance is on a part-time basis at a community college. Kane and Rouse (1995) show that earnings increase by 5 to 8 percent in response to a year of college courses, even if individuals do not complete a degree. The authors use an instrumental variable technique to address the issue of self-selection into community college and find that their results are not sensitive to the use of this technique. Leigh and Gill (1997) show that students receive similar earnings gains if they return to school after a period in the labor force or if they continue on to community college directly after high school.

These market returns provide an incentive for military members to continue their education in the military, but they may also encourage them to leave for full-time schooling or to take advantage of the civilian wage premium on their schooling. Additional schooling increases promotion opportunities in the military and the civilian sector, so it is unclear which opportunities rise faster. The military also offers substantial postservice educational benefits to military members that provide an incentive for them to complete their enlistment term and pursue educational opportunities on either a full- or part-time basis as a civilian.

Another piece of research of relevance to this report examines civilian employer-sponsored education. In this review, we do not discuss employer-provided on-the-job training or other on-site job training programs provided directly by the employer. Rather, we focus on employer-sponsored university education programs. The Bureau of Labor Statistics' Employee Benefits Survey of 1995–1997 shows that only about 20 percent of full-time employees are offered non-job-related educational assistance in medium and large private establishments. However, more than 60 percent of these employees are offered job-related educational assistance. About 65 percent of employees participate in job-related educational assistance programs and about 20 percent participate in non-job-related educational assistance. We are not aware of a civilian literature on the relationship between firm-sponsored educational assistance and retention at the firm.

Boesel and Johnson (1988) was the first study to systematically examine the relationship between TA and military retention. The authors merged military records on TA usage with personnel data collected in the 1985 DoD Survey. TA records were not centrally collected, so they contacted education offices at each military base to collect TA information for matched individuals at each assignment. Retention was based on continuation in the service between June 1986 and December 1987. They were unable to collect TA data for the Marine Corps.

Boesel and Johnson (1988) found that the retention rate for TA users was about 12 percentage points higher than for nonusers. They showed that TA usage was higher for members who were older, in higher pay grades, female, better educated, and of higher aptitude than for other members. The usage rate also varied substantially across services: 24.1 percent of airmen had used TA, compared with 10.4 and 5.2 percent of soldiers and sailors, respectively.[2]

The model used logit regression to examine how TA, pay grade, sex, race, aptitude, marital status, and service affiliation affected retention. The study approach, while novel at the time, has four weaknesses.

- **Unequal opportunities to use TA.** Since leavers are in the Navy for fewer months than stayers, they have less access to TA. This makes stayers inherently more likely to use TA than leavers, simply because they have a greater opportunity to use the program. Boesel and Johnson (1988) may simply be observing that TA usage rises along with the time eligible and incorrectly inferring that TA usage is linked to retention.

- **Unusual measure of retention.** The study focuses on retention over an 18-month window, but it does not distinguish between members leaving at the end of their term and those leaving during their term (i.e., attrition). Nearly a third of first-term mem-

---

[2]Members of the Army, Navy, and Air Force are referred to as soldiers, sailors, and airmen. Similarly, members of the Marine Corps are referred to as marines.

bers leave during their obligation as a result of adjustment or job performance problems. These losses are largely involuntary, and these members would not have been allowed to reenlist at the end of their term. These members struggle for some time before their separation and are unlikely to take college courses, so their inclusion may inappropriately inflate the effect of TA usage on retention.

- **Combined broad groups**. Boesel and Johnson (1988) estimate a single retention equation for all enlisted personnel in the Navy, Army, and Air Force. This construction forces the TA effect to be the same across very different groups. No a priori reason exists to expect TA usage to have the same effect in each service. Indeed, the large difference in TA rates across services suggests that the programs may have important service differences that should be controlled for. For instance, accessibility and incentives to take TA courses may differ between services. Therefore, the effect of TA on retention may be expected to differ by service. Similarly, the retention rate for senior members is much higher than that for first-term soldiers, but the model restricts TA to have a common effect across groups. Their average retention rate is 69 percent, compared with a typical first-term retention rate of 30 to 40 percent. Given the difference in the retention rates between these groups, we may expect the responsiveness of their retention rates to such factors as TA usage to differ.

- **TA usage treated as exogenous**. The statistical approach ignores the fact that TA usage may be jointly determined with retention. For example, members may use TA to enhance and improve their military skills or to prepare for a postmilitary career. Suppose that most members use TA to improve their military promotion prospects. Then, we might see a positive effect of TA usage on retention in this type of model, but the effect is capturing the indirect interest of the member in staying and not the direct effect of TA use on retention per se. This joint determination of TA and retention should be incorporated in the statistical model to avoid biasing the results.

We reestimated the Boesel and Johnson (1988) model with our data and found that their results were very sensitive to their modeling approach.[3] We considered retention of sailors and marines over the 18-month period from October 1994 through March 1996. As in the Boesel and Johnson (1988) study, the results show that marines and sailors who use TA during that period are 5 and 3 percentage points more likely than nonusers to remain in the military over this period. The typical leaver was eligible for TA for only half of the 18 months, however, so the higher TA rate for stayers may simply reflect their eligibility for the program over a longer period.

We estimated another model that looks at member retention in one period as a function of TA participation in a previous period. This approach mirrors Boesel and Johnson's model, but it looks at whether TA participation in one 18-month period predicts retention in the following 18-month period. We only consider members who are in the military for the entire 18-month initial window, so subsequent stayers and leavers all have equal access to TA. These results show that members who used TA were *less* likely to remain in the military: marines and sailors who use TA during the initial 18-month interval were 12 and 8 percentage points less likely to complete the next 18 months of military service. This result suggests that TA users are disproportionately leaving the military for full-time schooling or civilian job opportunities.

Garcia and Joy (1998) evaluated the effectiveness of the voluntary education program for the Navy. Voluntary education encompasses TA, PACE, and Academic Learning Centers (ALCs) that provide basic instruction in reading, writing, math, and science skills. Their approach improved on Boesel and Johnson (1988) by estimating a bivariate probit model of voluntary education usage and retention. This approach was designed to isolate the direct effects of TA usage on continuation in the Navy and avoid the possible bias in the earlier Boesel and Johnson (1988) study.

Garcia and Joy (1998) also improved on the earlier study by focusing on continuation for the FY 1992 cohort at the end of the first term as compared with the retention of all personnel at a point in time. Garcia and Joy (1998) found large positive effects of TA usage on retention. The probability of continuation for a sailor who does not

---

[3]The reestimation procedure and results are documented in Appendix A.

use TA was 31 percent, and this percentage rises by 6 percentage points for each 15 semester hours of college credit earned during the first term. They predicted that 43 percent of members with 30 credits will stay and 55 percent of members with 60 credits will stay. Using these estimates, they computed the cost-effectiveness of TA and argued that the program benefits were twice the associated costs.

Garcia and Joy (1998) found similar patterns of TA usage to the earlier Boesel and Johnson study (1988). They found that women, higher-aptitude, and better-educated (at accession) sailors were more likely to use TA than others. Sailors who enlisted at a younger age were less likely to use TA than members with some work experience before joining the Navy. Hispanics and Asian/Pacific Islanders were more likely to take college courses than otherwise comparable blacks or white non-Hispanics. They found that marital status had no statistically significant effect on TA use.

As in the Boesel and Johnson (1988) study, the Garcia and Joy (1998) approach is problematic because stayers and leavers have unequal access to TA. They focused on sailors who initially contracted for a four-year stay in the Navy. Their continuation measure contrasted sailors who reenlist or extend their enlistment for more than one year with sailors who "left before or on completion of their contracts." This approach means that leavers have substantially fewer months in the Navy than do stayers, so they inherently have much less opportunity to use TA.

A key factor in the Garcia and Joy (1998) analysis was the identification of their statistical model using an instrumental variable technique. To isolate TA effects on continuation, their model required some exogenous attribute that had a direct effect on TA usage and no direct effect on retention. Ideally, this attribute should independently affect only TA usage, not retention. In doing so, this attribute provides the analyst with independent variation of TA usage to be correlated with continuation. In Garcia and Joy (1998), this key variable was an indicator for whether the sailor participated in academic counseling on a ship.

We agree with the spirit of the Garcia and Joy (1998) approach and see the study as an improvement on the earlier study by Boesel and Johnson (1988). The study is misleading, however, because stayers have much greater access to TA than leavers, and this distorts the estimated effect of TA usage on continuation rates. In addition, the study has several other weaknesses that may bias its results.

- **Questionable identification of the model.** Sailors are likely to attend academic counseling because they are interested in taking a course, so counseling is not exogenous relative to TA usage. We suspect that participation in academic counseling on a ship may be directly related to retention, independent of TA, and this would bias the estimates presented in the study. In addition, the variable only applies to a portion of voluntary education users (i.e., those on ships) and does not apply to TA for shore-bound sailors. Finally, only 2 percent of sailors attended this type of orientation. Even if counseling had an exogenous effect on TA and had no direct effect on retention, this small proportion may distort the accuracy of the final results.

- **Predictions outside the range of TA usage.** The large effects of TA on retention are predicated on accumulating large numbers of college credits while in the Navy. They show that 15 college credits, relative to no college credits, increases retention from 31 percent to 37 percent. While this effect may seem large, the majority of sailors using TA earn far less than 15 credits over the first term.[4]

- **Study mixes effects of different program elements.** Garcia and Joy (1998) also combine the effects of TA, PACE, and ALCs in their study. This approach is potentially misleading because the goals and incentives for sailors to use the alternative programs may be very different. While Garcia and Joy do separate the effect of using different voluntary education programs on retention, they estimate a single combined equation for participation in any voluntary education program. This may be problematic because it artificially constrains the effects of demographic variables to have the same effect on the participation in each type of program. For example, sailors with some college are unlikely to

---

[4]The average credits for a TA user in the first term are not reported in the study. The voluntary education participation rate is reported as 15 percent. About 92 percent of voluntary education enrollments are for college courses. The average number of college credits is 1.23 per sailor. This suggests that the average college credits per first-term user are about 8.9.

use ALCs and dropouts are unlikely to use TA, but the model estimates an average effect of these education variables on voluntary education usage.

We reestimated the Garcia and Joy (1998) model to assess whether their approach is sensitive to the unequal access of stayers and leavers to TA.[5, 6] First, we mirrored Garcia and Joy's (1988) approach by focusing on four-year enlistees from the FY 1992 cohort and looked at four-year continuation rates, where losses include members who leave *on or before* the end of their enlistment term. The results show that TA users have continuation rates 5 percentage points higher than nonusers (30 percent of TA users stay as compared with 25 percent of nonusers).

Next, we considered reenlistment decisions at the end of the first term, where the sample is restricted to members who successfully completed their term. The deleted observations reflect attrition during the first term, and these early leavers had an average of 1.8 years of service at separation. The early leavers had much less opportunity to use TA because they did not complete their four-year term. Those members who completed their four-year term had equal access to TA. The results show that TA users have reenlistment rates 6 percentage points lower than those of nonusers.

Our findings show that the positive effect of TA in the Garcia and Joy (1988) study is driven by the inclusion in their sample of sailors who leave well before the end of their enlistment term. These sailors have much less opportunity to use TA than do sailors who complete their terms, because they are TA-eligible for substantially fewer months. When we consider sailors who have access to TA for an equal number of months, we find that TA users are less likely to stay than nonusers.

Garcia et al. (2002) also examine TA usage and continuation in the Navy, using the same data and approach as the Garcia and Joy (1998)

---

[5]We do not have data on PACE usage, so our results are not strictly comparable with those of Garcia and Joy (1998). PACE constitutes about 15 percent of voluntary education enrollments. Our results focus on the TA portion of the voluntary education program that pays for member enrollment in college courses.

[6]The details of the estimation are reported in Appendix B.

study. Garcia et al. (2002) show that the average TA user has a six-year completion rate that is 11 to 13 percentage points higher than the average sailor who does not use TA. Their sample is restricted to sailors who joined the Navy in FY 1992 and contracted to stay for two to four years.

This study has the same weakness as the Boesel and Johnson (1988) and Garcia and Joy (1998) studies—i.e., stayers have much greater opportunity to use TA than leavers—and this may contradict their inference that TA usage somehow induces greater retention. Military losses cluster at low years of service as unsuitable sailors are weeded out and dissatisfied sailors complete their initial enlistments and leave the Navy. In the FY 1992 cohort, the average sailor who leaves in the first six years is only in the Navy for 2.3 years. As a result, leavers may be less likely to use TA than stayers simply because they are eligible for the program for substantially fewer years. The key issue is whether sailors stay longer because they use TA (as Garcia et al. (2002) argue) or whether sailors are more likely to use TA *because* they stay longer.

We reestimated the Garcia et al. (2002) model for the FY 1992 cohort of sailors and found that TA users had continuation rates 12 percentage points higher than for comparable nonusers.[7] The result is misleading, because leavers have much less access to TA than stayers by virtue of their shorter time in the Navy.

We estimated an alternative model that examines whether sailors who completed a fixed interval of time (say, five years) and used TA during that interval have a different retention rate in the next year than do TA nonusers. This approach automatically fixes the time that members are eligible for TA and looks forward to see whether TA usage affects subsequent retention.

Our results show that the Garcia et al. (2002) findings are sensitive to the leavers having less access to TA than stayers. We find that sailors who use TA during their first five years in the military have sixth year retention rates 9 percentage points *lower* than those of comparable sailors who do not use TA. We also estimated fifth, fourth, and third-year continuation rates whether the eligibility window for TA usage

---

[7]A detailed discussion of the estimation is in Appendix C.

was four, three, and two years, respectively. In each case, we found that retention rates were 5 to 6 percentage points lower for TA users than for comparable nonusers. This result suggests that TA users are disproportionately leaving the Navy for full-time schooling or civilian opportunities.

EMPIRICAL METHODOLOGY

This research expands on the earlier studies and develops models to better disentangle the relationship between TA usage and retention. Our approach addresses two research questions. First, which factors determine servicemembers' tendency to take a college course and use TA? Second, does TA participation affect a servicemembers' tendency to reenlist?

Ideally, the effect of TA usage on retention could be measured in a controlled experiment in which members were randomly assigned eligibility for TA. This approach would isolate program effects, but an experiment is not feasible in this case, where the services have an ongoing TA program. We develop two models that allow us to estimate the effect of the TA usage on retention. First, we use a bivariate probit model to jointly estimate the factors that influence both TA usage and retention. This model ensures that servicemembers' characteristics that directly affect TA usage do not contaminate the effect of TA usage on retention. This model is similar to that of Garcia and Joy (1998) and Garcia et al. (2002). The second model is a propensity score model that compares the retention decisions of TA users with those of very similar matched observations for nonusers and interprets the difference in the retention rates as an estimate of the effect of TA usage on retention. This matched sampling or propensity score approach has been used recently in the evaluation of how a specific treatment, such as civilian job training, affects subsequent earnings. We have adapted this methodology to see how TA participation affects retention.

The bivariate probit model and the propensity score model are based on different assumptions. The bivariate probit model relies on assumptions about the distribution of the data and the validity of the variables that are assumed to affect TA usage but not retention. In contrast, the propensity score approach depends less on distributional assumptions. Using both the propensity score and the bivariate probit method verifies the robustness of our results to the assumptions implicit in the two models.

The analysis focuses on first-term enlistees who have successfully completed their term and are deciding whether to stay or leave the military. Members were excluded from our analysis if they were involuntarily separated from the military without completing their service obligation. The decision to stay in the military at the end of the term is modeled as a function of TA usage over the 24-month period prior to the retention decision point (the end of the initial enlistment) as well as various demographic and military characteristics. This approach avoids the problems of previous research in which the period of eligibility for TA usage differed across individuals in the analysis.

Bivariate Probit Model of TA Usage and Retention

Following earlier research, we expect that TA usage will vary substantially with the demographic and military characteristics of individual sailors and marines. Some types of individuals will have stronger interest in college classes than others. The model shows how demographic characteristics (i.e., age, aptitude, gender, and marital status) and military factors (i.e., occupation, deployment status, and assignment location) affect TA usage.

Several earlier studies have modeled first-term retention as a function of a member's demographic characteristics and military experiences (Warner and Solon, 1991; Buddin et al., 1992; and Hosek and Totten, 1998). This model is expanded to include data about whether the individual uses TA during the first term.

The primary analytic problem to be addressed in estimating the retention equation is the potential endogeneity of TA usage. We believe that TA usage is potentially endogenous or, in other words, confounded with other factors within the model. One reason for the endogeneity of TA usage is that individuals with higher ability (unmeasured by the analyst) may be more likely to take TA courses. Unmeasured individual ability may also directly affect reenlistment. Therefore, the estimate of the effect of TA on reenlistment in a model that does not account for the endogeneity of TA may be biased. Our bivariate probit model of TA usage and retention addresses this potential problem.

Several factors affect TA usage and have no direct effect on retention. These factors could be used to identify the statistical model and get unbiased estimates of how TA affects retention.

- **Access to college before enlistment.** We expect that some members have a stronger interest in college than others. The literature on college attendance suggests that individuals growing up near a four-year college are more likely to attend college than those who live far from a college (Card, 1993; Rouse, 1994; Kane and Rouse, 1999). While many of these students go directly to college, we expect that military members who grew up near a college may have a stronger interest or expectation in attending college (on average) than other members. Our model includes a measure of the distance between the members' home when they joined the military and the nearest four-year college to capture the effect of these possible differences in "tastes" for college.

- **Educational opportunities at base.** Military members have little choice about their base assignment and are probably unfamiliar with college course availability until they arrive at their base. If course availability is greater, we expect that members would be more likely to enroll and use TA. There is no corresponding reason to expect course availability to have a direct effect on retention. Our model includes a measure of the number of colleges offering courses at each member's base (the model also holds constant base size).

- **Time cost of college enrollment.** Some members live far from the base education center and may spend considerable driving time to attend a class. This time cost may vary considerably across members who live on and off base, but it may also be considerable for on-base members on some large bases. Members generally have little choice in the location of on-base housing, and the off-base choice for first-term members is dictated by cost considerations more than proximity to on-base college classes. Other things being equal, we expect that the probability of attending a class and using TA is inversely related to their time cost in getting to class. Unfortunately, we did not have this information available, so it is not included in our model. We did include information about whether the member lived on or off base, but we felt that this housing measure would affect retention directly as well as through its affect on TA usage.

In our model, we rely on the member's distance from a four-year college at accession and the number of colleges offering courses on their base as identifying, or instrumental, variables that are included in the TA equation and excluded in the retention equation.

Our complete model consists of a tuition equation and a first-term retention equation.[8] The tendency for TA usage is

$$TA_i^* = \beta_2 X_i + \delta Z_i + \varepsilon_{2i},$$

where the individual's tendency to take a TA course (denoted by TA_i^*) is modeled as a function of a (column) vector of observed variables, X_i, a (row) vector of unobserved parameters β_2, a set of variables that measure the member's "taste" for college classes and the TA opportunities available on the individual's base, Z_i and their corresponding parameters δ, and an unobserved random error ε_{2i}. The explanatory variables in X_i include the servicemember's demographic characteristics, such as age, sex, race, marital status, education, and Armed Force Qualification Test (AFQT) score categories.[9] X_i also includes variables on the servicemembers' occupation and months deployed during the year. Z_i is excluded from the reenlistment equation, because these variables have no direct effect on retention and affect retention only indirectly through their effect on TA usage. The subscript i denotes an individual. The variable TA_i^* is a continuous measure of the tendency to take a TA course, but the investigator observes only whether a course is taken, so the observed variable, TA_i is truncated as a zero-one variable:

$$TA_i = \begin{cases} 1 \text{ if } TA_i^* > 0 \\ 0 \text{ otherwise} \end{cases}$$

---

[8]A short explanation of the bivariate probit model is presented in this chapter, and a more detailed description appears in Appendix D.

[9]AFQT is scored on a percentile scale, based on a nationally representative sample of American youth. AFQT categories are based on ranges of the AFQT percentile score.

Retention is modeled as a function of the same set of X variables and TA usage. The tendency to reenlist is a latent (i.e., not directly observed) random variable. The individual's tendency to reenlist, denoted by R_i^*, is modeled as a function of a (column) vector of observed variables, X_i, a (row) vector of unobserved parameters β_1, an indicator variable that denotes whether or not the individual took a TA course, TA_i and its corresponding parameter g, and an unobserved random error ε_{1i}.

$$R_i^* = \beta_1 X_i + \gamma TA_i + \varepsilon_{1i}$$

The variable R_i^* is a continuous measure of the tendency to reenlist. In fact, the investigator only observes the action to reenlist, so the observed variable, R_i, is truncated as a zero-one variable:

$$R_i = \begin{cases} 1 \text{ if } R_i^* > 0 \\ 0 \text{ otherwise} \end{cases}$$

We estimate this two-equation system using a bivariate probit model that allows for possible error term correlation between the residuals in the TA and retention equations. Under the assumptions of the model, the parameter estimates are unbiased, and γ shows the direct effect of TA usage on retention. The model also estimates the underlying correlation between unobserved factors in the two equations. This correlation may be significant because some unmeasured factors that affect TA usage may also affect retention. Accounting for the correlation between the two equations also improves the precision of the model estimates. An example of a factor that may induce a correlation between TA usage and retention is a servicemember's taste for military life. Members who enjoy military life are likely to take TA courses to increase their promotion opportunities within the military. In addition, these members are less likely to leave the military. Therefore, servicemembers' tastes can induce a correlation between TA usage and retention.

We have no strong a priori expectation about how TA usage affects retention. TA usage is a military benefit, so users may have an extra incentive to stay in the military and take advantage of the program. College classes may also increase promotion speed and military wage growth. At the same time, however, the college skills transfer readily to the civilian sector, and this experience will increase civilian opportunities as well. Finally, some students may be frustrated by military schedules and assignments that interfere with college attendance, so they may leave to pursue a full-time college program. This option is enhanced by military education benefits that subsidize college training after the member leaves the military.

Propensity Score Model of How TA Affects Retention

We use a propensity score model as an alternative estimation strategy to measure the effect of TA usage on retention. This statistical methodology compares the retention behavior for a TA user with that for a matched nonuser (Rosenbaum and Rubin, 1985; Angrist, 1997; Heckman et al., 1997; Angrist, 1999; Dehejia and Wahba, 1999; Hirano et. al., 2000, and Ichimura and Taber, 2001). Ideally, we would like to know whether an individual who uses TA would have been more or less likely to stay in the military if they had not used TA. This type of comparison could be made if TA enrollment were random across military members. Then, the effect of the program on retention would be the difference in retention rate for the group with mandatory TA enrollment relative to the group that did not have mandatory TA enrollment.

The propensity score approach attempts to replicate an experimental design by comparing outcomes (retention) for otherwise very similar individuals. Individuals are aligned based on their predicted probability of using TA, and each user is matched with a nonuser with a similar probability of using TA. This matching of users and nonusers balances the two groups on the observed factors that affect TA. Only about 10 percent of members use TA during their first term, and we may expect that many nonusers are unlikely to take a college class (e.g., they have long deployments or low levels of education). These expected differences in TA users and nonusers suggest that the full set of TA nonusers is an inappropriate comparison group for TA users. The propensity score matching approach addresses this issue by linking observations with similar probabilities of using TA.

The model is estimated in two steps. The first step estimates the probability of TA usage as a function of demographic characteristics, military environment, proximity to a four-year college at accession, and number of colleges offering courses at the member's base. This is the same as the first equation in our bivariate probit model. From this equation, we predict the probability of TA usage based on each individual's X and Z variables. This prediction is called the propensity score. For each TA user, we find the nearest available nonuser in terms of propensity score. Finally, using the matched sample, we estimate the probability of retention as a function of the X variables and TA usage. The estimated effect of TA usage on retention is the coefficient of the TA variable in this retention equation.

The propensity score approach has two advantages over the bivariate probit model.

- The propensity score approach does not require a set of variables that affect TA and not retention as the bivariate probit model does. In our case, however, we have suitable information on access to college before enlistment and educational opportunities at the base that have a direct effect on TA usage and no direct effect on retention.

- This propensity approach does not make functional form restrictions on the error term correlation in the TA usage and retention equation. In the bivariate probit model, we assume that the unobserved factors affecting TA usage and retention are bivariate normal.

The disadvantage of the propensity score method is that it only adjusts for observed differences between TA users and nonusers. If these groups differ systematically in some unmeasured factors that affect retention, then the propensity score method might be misleading. The bivariate probit model is better suited to handing correlations in unobserved factors between the two equations. By using two different methodologies, the propensity score approach and the bivariate probit joint model, we are able to evaluate whether our estimates of the effect of TA usage on retention are robust to the estimation approach.

The propensity score method has been used in the evaluation of the effectiveness of civilian job-training programs. Researchers have struggled with the problem of trying to anticipate how federal expenditures on job training will affect the wages of low-wage earners. In many cases, databases contain information on the earnings of training participants before and after training, and the training effect is the measured gain in earnings after completing the course. The problem with this approach is that this measured effect may overstate the potential earnings gains of nonparticipants because the individuals with the highest potential gains were the first to use the program. Dehejia and Wahba (1999) show that the propensity score approach does very well in predicting outcomes for an experimental job-training design where the "true" effect is known from randomization.

DATA

Our analysis is based on the first-term retention decisions of enlisted personnel in the Navy and Marine Corps during FY 1997 and the first half of FY 1998. We focus on first-term retention for several reasons. First, we expect the pattern of TA usage may differ during the first term from that in the career force. Second, we believe that TA usage is likely to have the largest effect on retention for first-term members who may be in the process of choosing long-term careers.

We have obtained records of servicemembers' participation in the TA program for 24 months prior to their reenlistment decision. We restricted our analysis to individuals who had successfully completed their first term and were considering staying for a second term. The analysis file consists of two main components: monthly records on DoD personnel that include information on their individual demographics and military situation and course records for each course enrollment of a sailor or marine. We merge this information and some information from other sources to build our analysis file.

The initial personnel data file was built by the Defense Manpower Data Center (DMDC) and provides a month-by-month record of members during their enlistment term. The file contains information on servicemembers' demographics, pay grade, pay components, and deployment. The data also include information on the number of months remaining in the servicemember's enlistment term and whether or not a separation takes place. Following the methodology developed in Hosek and Totten (1998), we used annual measures of hostile deployment and total deployment based on pay information for Family Separation Allowance and Imminent Danger Pay during the year. Hosek and Totten (1998) note that these measures of deployment are imperfect proxies for deployment. However, they are the best available given the current data limitations.

The deployment information is especially pertinent to our analysis because work responsibilities make it difficult for members to take college courses during deployments. In recent years, the services have attempted to improve the access of deployed members to college through distance learning and enhanced PACE offerings. Nonetheless, the incentives and opportunities for enrolling in college classes are different during a deployment from when members are residing at their home base.

The second data source used in our analysis is the course enrollment and completion data from the Navy Campus Management Information System (NCMIS). These records are the basis for TA reimbursement, and, for all TA takers, they contain information on each course name, number of credits, university, and whether the course was successfully completed. Using the enlisted servicemembers' Social Security number, we merged the DMDC and the NCMIS data to create the analysis database.

One limitation of our database is that we do not have information on college classes taken through PACE while members are at sea.[10] These classes are not recorded in the NCMIS, and we were unable to obtain access to this information. We do know when the member was deployed or on a ship, however, so we can control for when the member had access to shore-based TA programs. In PACE, the service pays for 100 percent of enrollment costs, compared with 75 percent reimbursement under TA for members not at sea. In addition to these cost differences, members have work schedules and personal responsibilities during a sea deployment different from when they are in port or on shore duty, so the incentives for taking college courses are likely to vary considerably between PACE courses and those land-based courses covered by TA. For these reasons, our analysis focuses on the TA college courses for members not at sea.

We added several other variables to the database. First, we merge information on the number of schools offering courses at the servicemembers' current base. Second, using the servicemembers'

---

[10]About 15 percent of TA courses in the Navy are taken through PACE.

Zip code before enlistment, we merge information on the service-members' proximity to a four-year college before enlistment in the Navy or Marine Corps.

About 33 percent of sailors and 21 percent of marines reenlist at the end of their first enlistment term. The interservice gap reflects the Marine Corps' greater emphasis on a young, junior workforce and that it has a smaller career component than does the Navy. Figure 2.1 shows that the retention rate in each service varies little by whether the member used TA. This figure is a simple description of the retention pattern in the data and does not adjust for differences in member demographics and military experiences likely to affect both TA usage and retention. By this simple measure, we see that TA users have retention rates 2 percentage points lower than nonusers for both the Navy and Marine Corps.

TA usage does vary considerably across different types of sailors and marines. Figure 2.2 shows that the overall TA usage rate is 8 percent

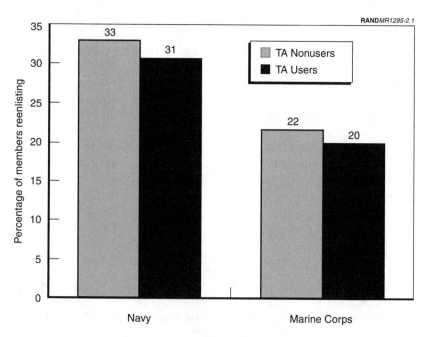

Figure 2.1—Patterns of First-Term Retention by TA Usage in the Navy and Marine Corps

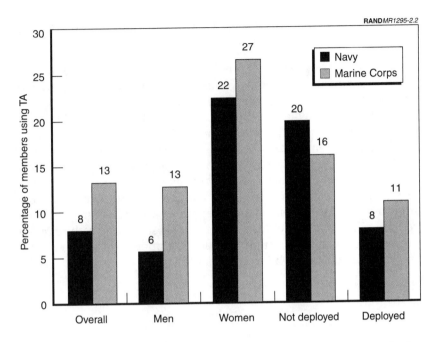

Figure 2.2—Patterns in TA Usage by Gender and Deployment Status in the Navy and Marine Corps

in the Navy, compared with 13 percent in the Marine Corps. The figure highlights differences in TA usage by gender and deployment status. Navy women are three times as likely to use TA as Navy men, and Marine Corps women are twice as likely to use TA as Marine Corps men. These gaps may indicate that women have much greater interest in college classes than men, but the difference in interest is confounded with such other factors as work and family responsibilities that may also affect TA usage. For example, Figure 2.2 also shows that deployed members are much less likely to use TA than nondeployed members. This reflects the extended work schedules during deployments, which leave members little time to enroll in a class. Women are much less likely to be deployed than men, however, so part of the gender gap in TA usage reflects differences in deployment by gender and part of the deployment gap in TA usage reflects gender composition by deployment status. Our statistical model uses a multivariate approach that disentangles these effects and isolates how each factor contributes to TA usage while holding constant other demographic and military factors.

Another interesting aspect of our data is that we have information on the number of credits earned over time. In early work, we considered whether the number of credits earned affected retention compared with a measure of whether the member used TA. We found that the usage measure was sufficient for the analysis because few members accumulated many credits. Among TA users, the median number of credits earned in the past 24 months was six semester hours in both services. These rates of course accumulation mean that members are making very slow progress toward the 60-semester hour requirement for an associate's degree or the 120-semester hour requirement for a bachelor's degree. For most members, their rate of credit accumulation through TA does not appear to put them on a path to earn a degree while in the military.

Chapter Three

RESULTS FOR THE MARINE CORPS

BIVARIATE PROBIT MODEL OF TA USAGE AND RETENTION

The parameter estimates for the bivariate probit model of TA and retention are reported in Table 3.1. The table reports the estimated effect of each characteristic on TA usage and retention, the estimated standard error of each effect, and the mean value for each characteristic. For continuous variables, such as age, the effect corresponds to the derivative of the probability of either TA usage or retention with respect to the characteristic. In other words, we measure the effect of a one-unit increase in the value of the characteristic on the outcome probability. For binary variables, such as female, the effect corresponds to the effect of the binary variable being one relative to it being zero on the outcome probability—i.e., the difference in the outcome for males relative to females. Consider the results for age (a continuous measure) and female (a discrete, indicator variable for whether the member is female). The table entries for age imply that the probability of TA usage rises 0.24 percentage points for each year of age, and retention rises 0.36 percentage point for each year of age. These effects are evaluated at the means of all other characteristics in the model. Both age effects are statistically insignificant, so age has no significant effect on either TA usage or retention. The table entries for female mean that female members are predicted to have TA usage and retention rates 6 and 4 percentage points higher, respectively, than their male counterparts. These effects are statistically significant and are marked with an asterisk in the table. Finally, the means in the last column show that the average age of marines at the first-term retention point is 21.8 and that only 3.6 percent of members are female.

Table 3.1

Bivariate Probit Model Results for TA Usage and First-Term Retention in the Marine Corps

Characteristic	TA Usage		First-Term Retention		
	dF/dX	Standard Error	dF/dX	Standard Error	Mean
TA Usage in Past Two Years			−0.0592	0.0687	0.1313
Age	0.0024	0.0015	0.0036	0.0026	21.8092
Female	0.0622*	0.0118	0.0422*	0.0146	0.0362
Black	−0.0187*	0.0080	0.1379*	0.0118	0.1193
Hispanic	0.0309*	0.0078	0.0514*	0.0102	0.1131
Asian/Pacific Islander	0.0986*	0.0220	0.1325*	0.0254	0.0193
Category 1 (AFQT 93–99 Percentile)	0.0754	0.0393	0.0185	0.0739	0.0286
Category 2 (AFQT 65–92 Percentile)	0.0457	0.0286	0.0456	0.0648	0.3242
Category 3a (AFQT 50–64 Percentile)	0.0225	0.0264	0.0331	0.0655	0.2662
Category 3b (AFQT 31–49 Percentile)	−0.0143	0.0249	0.0251	0.0649	0.3233
Non–High School Graduate	−0.0900*	0.0360	0.1810*	0.0620	0.0013
GED	−0.0239*	0.0093	−0.0164	0.0266	0.0157
Alternative Education Credential	−0.0334*	0.0117	−0.0257	0.0163	0.0200
Some College	0.0077	0.0133	−0.0043	0.0443	0.0084
Single Parent	−0.0081	0.0078	0.1386*	0.0310	0.0341
Married Parent	−0.0271*	0.0068	0.1928*	0.0220	0.1425
Married Nonparent	0.0011	0.0040	0.1425*	0.0127	0.2954
Joint Military Couple	0.0170	0.0111	0.0454*	0.0115	0.0285
Skilled Technical	0.0526*	0.0125	0.0613*	0.0173	0.1271
Support and Administrative	0.1125*	0.0121	0.0784*	0.0174	0.1672
Electrical/Mechanical	0.0248	0.0128	0.0676*	0.0136	0.1547
Craftsmen, Service, and Supply Handlers	0.0357*	0.0142	0.0384*	0.0108	0.2132
Number of Deployments in Past Two Years	−0.0219*	0.0037	0.0190*	0.0055	0.8250
Months Deployed in Past Two Years	0.0014	0.0009	−0.0039*	0.0008	3.5226

Table 3.1—Continued

Characteristic	TA Usage		First-Term Retention		
	dF/dX	Standard Error	dF/dX	Standard Error	Mean
Lives in Off-Base Housing	0.0088	0.0047	−0.0729*	0.0083	0.2938
Retention Decision in FY 1997	0.0146*	0.0057	−0.0639*	0.0125	0.2990
Stationed Overseas (except Japan)	0.2976*	0.0511	0.0622	0.0474	0.0064
Stationed in Japan	0.0294*	0.0078	0.1192*	0.0128	0.0625
Size of Base (Logarithm of Enlisted/10,000)	0.0018	0.0050	−0.0173*	0.0040	−0.0971
Distance to Four-Year College	−0.0002	0.0001			21.5381
Number of Schools at Base	0.0080*	0.0023			2.0817
Proportion Staying at End of First Term					0.2136
Correlation (ρ)			0.0358	0.1547	
Sample Size					23585

NOTE: The estimated effects (dF/dX) correspond to changes in the probability relative to the excluded reference category for discrete variables and the derivative of the probability for continuous variables. Entries with asterisks are associated with coefficients that are significant at the $\alpha = 0.05$ confidence level.

The reference categories for demographic variables in the model are male, white non-Hispanic, test category 4 (10–30 percentile), high school diploma graduate, and single with no children. The reference groups for military characteristics are combat arms occupation, on-base housing, retention decision in FY 1998, stationed at U.S. base, and not using TA in the past two years.

TA does not have a statistically significant effect on the probability of a Marine Corps member reenlisting at the end of his or her first term. The results in Table 3.1 show that members who use TA are about 6 percentage points less likely to stay in the Marine Corps than are comparable others who do not use TA. This effect is measured imprecisely, however, and the estimated effect is not significantly different from zero.

The results do not provide support for the hypothesis that TA usage fosters or enhances retention. In the Marine Corps, the TA program has a neutral effect on retention. Of course, the program may have other benefits in term of enhanced recruiting or providing a productive outlet for members' off-duty time. These benefits may (or may not) outweigh the costs of the program, but the TA program is not working as a retention magnet for the Marine Corps.

The results also show a small and insignificant correlation between the TA equation and the retention equation. Unobserved factors that affect whether an individual uses TA are not correlated with unobserved factors in the retention equation. The model estimates this correlation to allow for the possibility that unmeasured variables might distort or bias the estimated effects and to increase the precision of the estimates

The remainder of this chapter describes what types of recruits use TA and what factors are related to reenlisting in the Marine Corps at the end of the first term.

TA Usage

TA usage varies somewhat across the basic demographic characteristics of marines. Women have TA usage rate 6 percentage points higher than otherwise comparable men. Asian/Pacific Islander and Hispanic members are more likely to use TA than are either black or white, non-Hispanic members: holding constant other factors at the means, the predicted TA usage percentages for Asian/Pacific Islanders, Hispanics, blacks, and white non-Hispanics are 23, 14, 10, and 12, respectively. Age has no significant effect on TA usage.

TA usage varies little with member aptitude and education. TA usage is highest for members in the highest AFQT percentiles (category 1, AFQT percentile 93 to 99), but the usage rate does not vary significantly across test score categories. Non–high school graduates, GED certificate holders, and marines with alternative education credentials have TA usage rates 9, 2, and 3 percentage points lower than members with a traditional high school diploma or some college. About 95 percent of marines were high school diploma graduates with no college training, however.

TA usage varies little with member marital or parental responsibilities. TA usage is about 3 percentage points lower for married parents than for single nonparents (the reference category). Single parents and married nonparents are no more or less likely to use TA than are single nonparents. Members who are married to military members (joint military) are no more likely to use TA than other married members. About 45 percent of marines are married by the end of the first term, while the average age is only 21.8 years.

Figure 3.1 shows that TA usage varies widely with member occupation.[1] Marines in functional support and administrative jobs are 2.5 times as likely to use TA as comparable marines in combat jobs. This difference may reflect greater interest in college courses by members in these occupations, but the difference also reflects greater oppor-

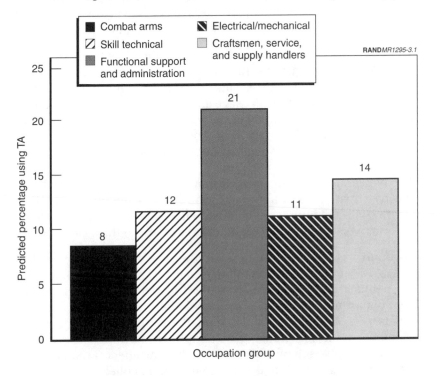

Figure 3.1—Predicted TA Usage by Occupation Group in the Marine Corps

---

[1]Occupation groups are based on one-digit DoD occupation codes, where combat arms (infantry, gun crews, and seamanship specialists) jobs are coded 0, skill technical jobs are coded 1 through 4 (electronic equipment repairmen, communications and intelligence specialists, health care specialists, and other technical and allied specialists), functional support and administration jobs are coded 5, electrical/mechanical jobs are coded 6, and craftsmen, service, and supply handler jobs are coded 7 and 8.

tunity to enroll in classes. Support and administrative jobs have more regular work schedules than do combat jobs, and this schedule makes it easier for these members to attend classes. Members in skilled technical, electrical/mechanical, and craftsmen, service, and supply handler jobs have TA usage rates 3 to 6 percentage points higher than comparable combat marines, but members in these occupations are substantially less likely to use TA than those in functional support and administrative jobs. These large occupation differences in TA participation are interesting and suggest that even after controlling for deployment status (discussed below), differential interest in or availability for TA courses by occupation may exist.

The model includes two measures of members' deployment status over the past two years: the number of deployments and the number of months deployed. The results show that the number of months deployed does not affect TA usage after controlling for the number of deployments. About 45 percent of the marines had no deployment, and their predicted TA usage is 14.9 percent. Another 32 and 19 percent of members had one or two deployments in the past two years, and the TA usage percentages are 11.3 and 8.7 for these two groups. The typical deployment time for marines with some deployment in the past two years is about six months. Deployment time rises slightly with the number of deployments, but 75 percent of deployed marines were deployed for eight months or less in the past two years.

Location has some bearing on whether the member takes college classes. Members assigned to Japan have TA usage rates 3 percentage points higher than marines in the United States. Less than 1 percent of marines are assigned overseas other than to Japan, but their TA usage rate is 29 percent higher than for marines in the U.S. Members in off-base housing are about 1 percent more likely to use TA than members in on-base housing, but the effect is not quite statistically significant. Finally, we see that more college opportunities at the base are associated with greater college attendance. For comparably sized bases, the model predicts that an additional school offering classes at the base increases TA usage by about 1 percentage point.

We predicted that access to a four-year college before joining with marines would affect TA usage. The results show that individuals who grew up closer to a college are more likely to use TA than other individuals. A 30-mile increase in the distance from a four-year college is associated with a 0.5 percentage point decrease in the TA usage. This effect is not significant for the two-tailed test at $\alpha = 0.05$ confidence level (as reported in the table), but the estimated effect is significant for the null hypothesis that TA usage declines with distance from a four-year college.

First-Term Retention

Retention varies considerably across several of the demographic groups in the analysis. The retention rates for women are 4 percentage points higher than for comparable men. Only about 16 percent of white non-Hispanics reenlist, but reenlistment rate is 14, 5, and 13 percentage points higher for blacks, Hispanics, and Asian/Pacific Islanders, respectively

AFQT category and education have little bearing on retention. Non–high school graduates are significantly more likely to stay than others, but this group was only about 0.1 percent of marines at the first-term retention point.

Marriage and parenthood are both associated with a higher likelihood of marine retention. Single parents have retention rates 14 percentage points higher than do single members without children. The retention of married nonparents and parents is 14 and 19 percentage points higher, respectively, than for similar single nonparents. Joint members (i.e., those married to military members) are even more likely to stay: They have retention rates 5 percentage points higher than otherwise comparable married members.

Retention varies somewhat with military occupation and deployment status during the first term. Retention is lowest in combat jobs and highest in support and administration. Retention rises by 1 percentage point per deployment, but it falls with the number of months deployed (about 2 percentage points per six-month deployment). This is consistent with the Hosek and Totten (1998) finding that retention rises with some deployment but falls for long deployments. Hosek and Totten (1998) argue that members are enthusiastic about using their training for a deployment, but they become frustrated by too frequent or protracted deployments.

Marines in off-base housing are about 7 percent less likely to stay than those living on-base. The military housing allowance covers most of the housing expenses for off-base housing, but members paid about 15 percent of their housing expenses in the period of our study. On-base housing and utilities are of no cost to members, but there is generally a one- to two-year waiting list for on-base housing (Buddin et. al., 1999). These extra out-of-pocket expenses for off-base members may explain why they are less likely to stay.

PROPENSITY SCORE MODEL OF HOW TA AFFECTS RETENTION

The propensity score was estimated from a probit regression of TA usage on the X and Z variables discussed above. The specification was identical to the first equation in the bivariate probit model. The average predicted TA usage rate for nonusers was 12.6 percent, compared with 16.5 for users. Figure 3.2 shows the median and interquartile range of the predictions for TA nonusers and users. The figure shows substantial differences in the predictions for the two groups, but substantial overlap also takes place in the distributions, which suggests that it should be easy to identify matches where the predictions are comparable for users and nonusers.

Table 3.2 shows that TA users and nonusers are not very similar in demographic or military characteristics before matching. The second column shows the t-statistic associated with the two-tailed test that the prematching mean of each demographic and military characteristic is the same for TA users as for nonusers. The means are significantly different from one another for most of the characteristics in the model. The profile of a TA user is much different from that of a nonuser. The dissimilarity between TA users and nonusers provides empirical justification that simply comparing the retention for TA users and nonusers is unlikely to provide the correct estimate of the effect of TA usage on retention. This demonstrates a need for a more complex modeling approach, such as the propensity score methodology or the bivariate probit model.

The matching process is used to select a nonuser record very similar to each user record. The third column in Table 3.2 shows the differences in means after matching are insignificant for all characteristics

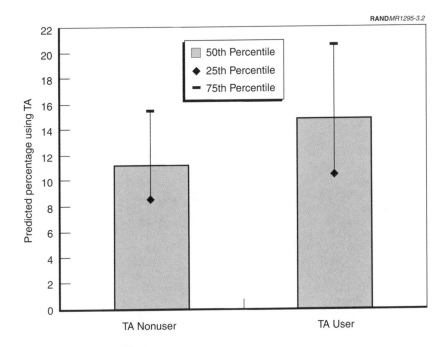

RAND*MR1295-3.2*

Figure 3.2—Predicted Probability of Using TA for Users and Nonusers in
the Marine Corps

in the model. Matching allows us to construct a sample of TA users
and nonusers that is similar across characteristics.

After picking the matched sample, we estimated a probit regression
model of first-term retention as a function of the X variables in the
model and TA participation. The results show that TA users have
first term retention rates 4.4 percentage points lower than members
who do not participate in the TA program.[2] Unlike the results from
the bivariate probit model, the negative effect of TA usage on retention is statistically significant in the propensity score model. The
statistical significance of the effect of TA usage on retention using the
propensity score approach is a result of the greater precision (smaller

---

[2]The estimated dF/dx is –0.0438 with a standard error of 0.0058. The 95 percent confidence interval for the estimated effect is from –0.0551 to –0.0324.

Table 3.2

Two-Tailed T-Test of Covariate Means (TA Users Minus Nonusers) Before and After Matching for the Marine Corps

Characteristic	Before Matching	After Matching
Age	1.33	0.11
Female	12.03*	−1.14
Black	−2.85*	1.52
Hispanic	4.09*	0.15
Asian/Pacific Islander	7.17*	0.41
Category 1 (AFQT 93–99 Percentile)	5.14*	−0.43
Category 2 (AFQT 65–92 Percentile)	8.82*	0.93
Category 3a (AFQT 50–64 Percentile)	0.58	0.51
Category 3b (AFQT 31–49 Percentile)	−12.77*	−0.84
Non–High School Graduate	−1.59	1.00
GED	−1.40	−1.05
Alternative Education Credential	−2.53*	0.77
Some College	2.27*	−0.34
Single Parent	0.23	−0.74
Married Parent	−5.27*	−0.44
Married Nonparent	2.38*	−0.22
Joint Military Couple	6.96*	0.97
Skilled Technical	3.36*	−1.23
Support and Administrative	17.43*	0.54
Electrical/Mechanical	−2.89*	−1.15
Craftsmen, Service, and Supply Handlers	−2.20*	0.57
Number of Deployments in Past Two Years	−13.06*	−0.36
Months Deployed in Past Two Years	−9.11*	−0.32
Lives in Off-Base Housing	1.06	−0.90
Retention Decision in FY 1997	4.21*	0.13
Stationed Overseas (except Japan)	9.70*	0.49
Stationed in Japan	4.45*	−1.36
Size of Base (in Logarithms)	−6.39*	1.00
Distance to Four-Year College	−2.56*	0.24
Number of Schools at Base	0.76	−0.89

NOTE: Entries with asterisks are associated with differences in means that are significant at the $\alpha = 0.05$ confidence level.

estimated standard error) obtained by using this approach. This result suggests that TA users are prone to leave the Marine Corps for civilian alternatives.

SUMMARY

Figure 3.3 summarizes our findings on TA usage and first-term retention for the Marine Corps. The unadjusted results show that TA users have reenlistment rates 2 percentage points lower than those of nonusers. These raw tabulations are a misleading indication of how TA affects retention because some types of members may be inherently prone to use TA and stay. The bivariate probit and propensity score models were used to isolate the direct contribution of TA usage to reenlistment. The results of the two models are similar.

- The bivariate probit model shows that marines who use TA have retention rates 6 percentage points lower than nonusers.

- The propensity score model shows that reenlistment rates for TA users are 4 percentage points lower than for nonusers.

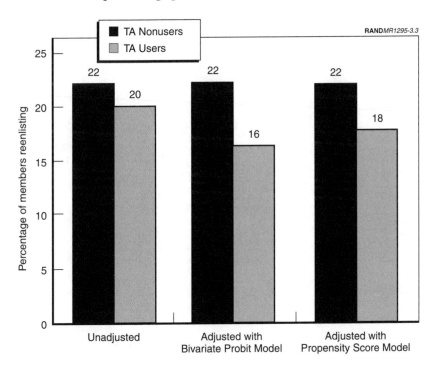

Figure 3.3—Estimated Effect of TA Usage on First-Term Reenlistment in the Marine Corps

The two models provide consistent evidence that TA users are prone to leave the Marine Corps for civilian employment or schooling alternatives.

Chapter Four

RESULTS FOR THE NAVY

BIVARIATE PROBIT MODEL OF TA USAGE AND RETENTION

Table 4.1 presents the results from the bivariate probit model for the Navy. The results show that TA users in the Navy are less likely to reenlist than similar nonusers. Table 4.1 shows that the probability of staying in the Navy at the end of the first term is 9 percentage points lower for sailors participating in TA than for other sailors. While TA may be an important recruiting incentive, our result suggests that TA users are prone to leave the Navy for civilian employment or schooling opportunities.

We explored the sensitivity of the model to the identifying variables in the model (distance to a four-year college at accession and the number of schools available at the member's base). We found that the results were stable for alternative specifications that relied on either variable individually for identification.

The error term correlation between the TA and retention equation is 0.12, but this correlation is not statistically significant. By adjusting for this correlating in the model, we allowed for the possibility that unobserved factors affecting TA usage might also affect retention and bias the estimated parameters. The results suggest that this potential bias is not substantial. The bivariate probit model also improves the efficiency of the model estimates.

About 8 percent of sailors use TA during the 24 months before their retention decision, compared with the 13 percent usage rate for the Marine Corps. The lower usage rate in the Navy reflects in part that many sailors are assigned to a ship. These seabound sailors have

Table 4.1

Bivariate Probit Model Results for TA Usage and First-Term Retention in the Navy

| Characteristic | TA Usage | | First-Term Retention | | |
	dF/dX	Standard Error	dF/dX	Standard Error	Mean
TA Usage in Past Two Years			−0.0892*	0.0393	0.0804
Age	0.0009	0.0006	0.0092*	0.0012	23.8702
Female	0.0607*	0.0077	0.0239	0.0142	0.1433
Black	−0.0042	0.0031	0.1967*	0.0092	0.1860
Hispanic	0.0228*	0.0045	0.0651*	0.0103	0.1044
Asian/Pacific Islander	0.0211*	0.0079	0.1925*	0.0153	0.0380
Category 1 (AFQT 93–99 Percentile)	0.0473*	0.0087	0.0534*	0.0155	0.0253
Category 2 (AFQT 65–92 Percentile)	0.0238*	0.0038	0.0063	0.0057	0.3294
Category 3a (AFQT 50–64 Percentile)	0.0097*	0.0030	0.0018	0.0053	0.2537
Non–High School Graduate	−0.0208*	0.0081	0.0522*	0.0238	0.0122
GED	−0.0241*	0.0081	0.0083	0.0187	0.0153
Alternative Education Credential	−0.0105	0.0068	0.0244	0.0225	0.0252
Some College	−0.0093	0.0067	−0.0519*	0.0195	0.0176
Single Parent	−0.0300*	0.0031	0.0973*	0.0161	0.0599
Married Parent	−0.0339*	0.0028	0.1372*	0.0196	0.1186
Married Nonparent	−0.0184*	0.0030	0.0971*	0.0149	0.2673
Joint Military Couple	−0.0049	0.0055	0.0490*	0.0172	0.0279
Skilled Technical	0.0272*	0.0043	0.1797*	0.0115	0.2469
Support and Administrative	0.0463*	0.0048	0.1866*	0.0102	0.1244
Electrical/Mechanical	−0.0073*	0.0030	0.0706*	0.0128	0.3169
Craftsmen, Service, and Supply Handlers	−0.0060	0.0056	0.1003*	0.0122	0.0981
Number of Deployments in Past Two Years	−0.0148*	0.0031	0.0194*	0.0065	1.4431
Months Deployed in Past Two Years	0.0000	0.0006	−0.0036	0.0021	5.5604
Lives in Off-Base Housing	0.0215*	0.0043	0.0039	0.0103	0.3390
Retention Decision in FY 1997	−0.0039	0.0027	−0.0004	0.0060	0.7585

Table 4.1—Continued

| Characteristic | TA Usage | | First-Term Retention | | |
	dF/dX	Standard Error	dF/dX	Standard Error	Mean
Stationed Overseas	0.0377*	0.0114	0.1020*	0.0320	0.0273
Assigned to a Ship	–0.0471*	0.0113	–0.0431*	0.0199	0.7223
Size of Base (Logarithm of Enlisted/10,000)	–0.0062*	0.0020	–0.0111*	0.0041	0.2141
Distance to Four-Year College	–0.0002*	0.0001			21.2623
Number of Schools at Base	–0.0047	0.0025			3.2596
Proportion Staying at End of First Term					0.3273
Correlation (ρ)			0.1215	0.0802	
Sample Size					32,712

NOTE: The estimated effects (dF/dX) correspond to changes in the probability relative to the excluded reference category for discrete variables and the derivative of the probability for continuous variables. Entries with asterisks are associated with coefficients significant at the $\alpha = 0.05$ confidence level.

The reference categories for demographic variables in the model are male, white non-Hispanic, test category 3b (31–49 percentile) or 4 (10–30 percentile), high school diploma graduate, and single with no children. The reference groups for military characteristics are combat arms occupation, on-base housing, retention decision in FY 1998, stationed at U.S. base, not assigned to a ship, and not using TA in the past two years.

long work schedules, so they may take fewer courses. Afloat courses are covered through PACE, but we have no record of these. Our analysis focuses on shore-based participation in TA that reimburses sailors for 75 percent of tuition costs. The results are adjusted for several factors associated with the limited opportunity of ship crews to take TA classes (e.g., assignment to a ship, number of deployments, and time deployed in the past 24 months). With these controls, we are able to isolate how various factors affect the tendency of a member to use TA.

Our results are at odds with the Garcia and Joy (1998) and Garcia et al. (2002) studies that TA users are more likely to stay in the Navy than nonusers. As shown in Chapter Two, however, the result from each study reflected the authors' use of an approach that failed to adjust for the period that stayers/leavers were eligible for TA. When we considered members with equal eligibility for TA in some initial period, we consistently found that TA users were less likely to stay in a subsequent period.

The remainder of this chapter examines how demographic and military characteristics affect TA usage and first-term retention.

TA Usage

TA usage patterns across basic demographic groups are similar for sailors and marines. TA usage for Hispanic and Pacific/Islander sailors is about 2 percentage points higher than for other sailors. Women are much more likely to use TA than comparable men: A woman is 6 percent more likely to take college classes than a man with similar demographic and military (i.e., this effect is after adjusting for ship assignment and deployment status) characteristics. As with the Marine Corps, age has no statistically significant effect on TA usage.

Aptitude and education levels related positively to TA usage in the Navy. TA usage is 1, 2, and 5 percentage points higher for sailors in AFQT categories 3a, 2, and 1, respectively, than for sailors in the lower AFQT categories. Non–high school graduates and sailors with a GED have TA usage rates about 2 percentage points below those of high school diploma graduates. The results show that members with some college before enlisting are no more likely to take college classes in the Navy than sailors with no college experience.

Family responsibilities are a minor disincentive to college enrollment. Parents (single or married) are less likely to take classes than are nonparents, but the difference in usage rate is only 3 percentage points. Similarly, married sailors with no children are 2 percentage points less likely to take college classes than are single nonparents.

Occupational differences in TA usage are much smaller in the Navy than in the Marines. Sailors in support and administrative jobs are most likely to use TA, and members in electrical/mechanical jobs are least likely to use TA. The range of probabilities across occupations is only about 5 percentage points, however.

The results suggest that heightened work pace during deployments may make it difficult to schedule college classes. The results show that TA usage over the 24-month period falls by about 1.5 percentage points per deployment. After controlling for the number of deployments, the length of deployment does not affect TA usage.

A surprising result is that TA usage for members in off-base housing is 2 percentage points higher than for members living on base. We had expected lower usage rates because sailors in off-base housing might be reluctant to return to the base for college classes. The result is puzzling because it suggests that proximity is inversely related to enrollment in college classes. One possible explanation is that most Navy-owned housing is not located in the community and not on the base itself (Buddin et. al., 1999). As a result, sailors in Navy housing (so-called "on-base housing") may actually be no closer to education centers than sailors living in private housing.

Assignment patterns have an important influence on TA usage. About 72 percent of the sailors in our data are assigned to a ship. Ship assignments detract from TA usage because members use PACE during sea deployments and because sailors have periods of intense work activity during the Interdeployment Training Cycle (IDTC). Even after controlling for deployment status, sailors assigned to a ship are 5 percentage points less likely to participate in TA than comparable other sailors. In contrast, sailors stationed overseas for shore duty have TA participation rates about 4 percentage points higher than other members.

As expected, sailor access to college before accession is related to TA usage in the Navy. Members who grew up near a four-year college are more likely to enroll in a college course while on active duty than are members who did not live near a college. These sailors have greater interest in college and pursue their education while in the Navy.

The number of schools at the Navy base did not have a statistically significant effect on TA usage. This variable behaves differently in the Navy and Marine Corps models. Number of schools is a proxy for college opportunities at the base, and the proxy seems to work poorly in the Navy. Better measures of college opportunities on different bases should be constructed for future analyses.

First-Term Retention

Navy retention varies substantially across demographic groups. Older sailors are more likely to stay than others: Each year increment in age is associated with a 1 percentage point increase in retention. Other things being equal, white non-Hispanics are much less likely to stay than other racial and ethnic groups. The retention rates for blacks, Hispanics, and Asian/Pacific Islanders are estimated as 20, 7, and 19 percentage points higher, respectively, than for otherwise comparable white non-Hispanics. No significant difference in retention exists for men and women at the first-term retention point.

Preservice education and aptitude have little effect on first-term retention in the Navy. Retention rates for category 1 sailors are 5 percentage points higher than for category 3b and 4. Only 3 percent of sailors are in category 1, however, and retention varies insignificantly across the broad range of scores achieved by most sailors. Non–high school graduates have retention rates 5 percentage points higher than high school diploma graduates. Sailors with some college before enlisting have retention rates about 5 percentage points lower than graduates with no college.

As in the Marine Corps, single sailors are less likely to stay than either married members or parents. Single parents and married nonparents are about 10 percentage points more likely to stay in the Navy than are single nonparents. Married parents have retention rates 14 percentage points higher than those of singles without dependents.

Retention rates vary substantially by occupation group. Sailors in combat jobs are much less likely to stay than counterparts in noncombat jobs. Support and administrative and electrical/mechanical jobs have retention rates about 18 percentage points higher than for combat jobs.

Retention decisions are sensitive to sailors' assignment patterns during the first term. Other things being equal, ship assignments reduce retention by 4 percentage points relative to shore assignments. Members enjoy the opportunity to use their training during a deployment, so retention rises 2 percentage points per deployment. Similarly, overseas shore assignments are popular, and sailors with these assignments have retention rates 10 percentage points higher than members with domestic shore assignments.

PROPENSITY SCORE MODEL OF HOW TA AFFECTS RETENTION

The first step in estimating the propensity score model for the Navy is to estimate a probit equation for TA usage. TA usage is modeled as a function of sailor characteristics and military experiences as reported in the TA equation of the bivariate probit model. Figure 4.1 shows the broad range of predicted TA usage based on this probit regression. The median predicted TA rate is six times greater for TA users (18 percent) than for nonusers (3 percent). The variance in the predicted rate for users is also much larger than for nonusers. These

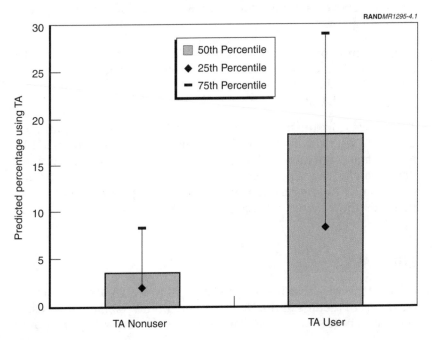

Figure 4.1—Predicted Probability of Using TA for Users and Nonusers in the Navy

differences mean that a direct comparison of retention rates for TA users and nonusers may be confounded by the set of factors that affect TA usage.

TA users are quite different from nonusers in terms of most of the demographic and military variables in the model. Table 4.2 shows that the prematching means and proportions differ substantially for nearly all variables in the model. Among the largest differences:

- 40 percent of TA users are female, compared with only 12 percent of nonusers.

- 32 percent of TA users are assigned to a ship compared with 76 percent of nonusers.

- The typical TA participant was deployed for 2.5 months in the past two years compared with 5.8 months for the typical non-participant.

The matching process pairs TA users with similar nonusers, so the differences in means for the covariates diminish substantially. The third column shows no significant differences in covariate means for the matched dataset.

The results from the propensity score model show that the probability of a TA user staying in the Navy at the end of the first term is 10.8 percentage points lower than for a comparable sailor who did not participate in TA.[1] This estimated effect is similar in magnitude and significance to our results from the bivariate probit model. Both methods show that the effect of TA usage on retention is large and negative.

SUMMARY

Figure 4.2 shows that first-term sailors who use TA are consistently less likely to reenlist in the Navy than are nonusers. The unadjusted numbers indicate that reenlistment rates are 2 percentage points

---

[1]The estimated dF/dX is –0.1079 with a standard error of 0.0163. The 95 percent confidence interval for the estimated effect is from –0.1399 to –0.0759.

Table 4.2

Two-Tailed T-Test of Covariate Means (TA Users Minus Nonusers) Before and After Matching for the Navy

Characteristic	Before Matching	After Matching
Age	3.73*	-1.35
Female	39.97*	0.03
Black	-2.91*	-0.44
Hispanic	3.99*	-0.57
Asian/Pacific Islander	2.97*	0.52
Category 1 (AFQT 93–99 Percentile)	5.99*	-0.60
Category 2 (AFQT 65–92 Percentile)	11.21*	0.95
Category 3a (AFQT 50–64 Percentile)	-0.70*	0.58
Non–High School Graduate	-2.80*	-0.65
GED	-3.23*	0.65
Alternative Education Credential	-2.90*	0.67
Some College	5.07*	0.24
Single Parent	-1.54	-1.47
Married Parent	-8.16*	-0.80
Married Nonparent	5.00*	0.33
Joint Military Couple	10.55*	-0.74
Skilled Technical	18.93*	-0.79
Support and Administrative	17.27*	0.92
Electrical/Mechanical	-17.81*	0.87
Craftsmen, Service, and Supply Handlers	-8.87*	-0.63
Number of Deployments in Past Two Years	-37.22*	0.74
Months Deployed in Past Two Years	-35.09*	1.32
Lives in Off-Base Housing	15.76*	-1.27
Retention Decision in FY 1997	-2.16*	-0.51
Stationed Overseas	30.38*	1.35
Assigned to a Ship	-48.98*	0.50
Size of Base (in Logarithms)	-30.10*	1.44
Distance to Four-Year College	-4.58*	-0.40
Number of Schools at Base	18.38*	0.13

NOTE: Entries with asterisks are associated with differences in means that are significant at the $\alpha = 0.05$ confidence level.

lower for TA users than for nonusers. The results from the two models adjust for differences in demographic and military characteristics of sailors that affect their retention and TA usage. The model results isolate the contribution of TA usage to reenlistment. The bivariate probit model results show that 25 percent of TA users reenlist in the

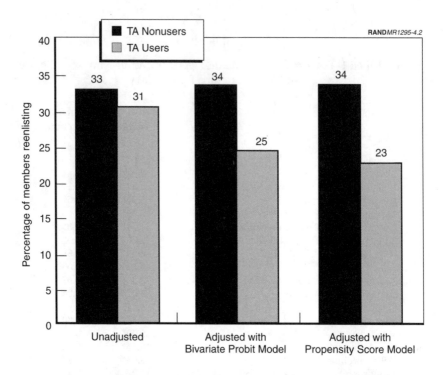

Figure 4.2—Estimated Effect of TA Usage on First-Term Reenlistment in the Navy

Navy, compared with 34 percent of nonusers. The gap between users and nonusers rose to 11 percentage points in the propensity score model. The similarity of the results for the two models suggests that the findings are robust to key modeling assumptions.

Chapter Five

CONCLUSIONS

In this report, we examined the effect of TA usage on first-term retention. In addition, we studied the factors that affect TA usage for marines and sailors. We found that several demographic and service factors have an impact on TA usage.

- **Basic demographic factors**. TA usage was higher for women and minorities than for other members. Age and education level had little effect on TA usage. Higher-aptitude sailors were more likely to use TA than other, but aptitude did not affect the TA participation of marines. Marriage and parenthood both decreased the likelihood that a sailor would use TA. Similarly, marines who are married parents were less likely to enroll in a college class than other marines.

- **Occupation**. TA use varies substantially with member occupation. In both services, TA usage was higher for skilled technical and support and administrative jobs than for other occupations. These occupation differences reflect the unpredictability of some occupations' work schedules, which makes it more difficult to schedule and complete a college class. Also, the members in jobs with predictable schedules might have greater interest in college enrollments.

- **Military assignment**. Members with overseas assignments are more likely to use TA than comparable others with a domestic assignment. Deployments decrease TA use. Sailors assigned to ships were less likely to use TA than other sailors. Seabound sailors can take classes through PACE during scheduled deployments, but ship crews have lower TA use even after controlling for deployment time, because of arduous work schedules during the IDTC.

These patterns of use reflect different opportunities for some types of members to take college classes as well as different interest in pursuing higher education.

TA usage does not increase the likelihood of marines or sailors reenlisting at the end of their first term. In the Marine Corps, the results from the propensity score model show that the typical TA user has a retention rate 4.4 percentage points lower than a comparable marine who did not participate in TA. The estimated effect from the bivariate probit model was a similar –5.9 percentage points for TA usage, but this effect was imprecisely measured and was not statistically different from zero. In the Navy, the bivariate probit results indicate that TA users had retention rates 8.9 percentage points lower than nonusers. The propensity score results indicate that the TA effect on retention is –10.8 percentage points. The negative effects are significantly different from zero for both Navy models.

Our results are at odds with those of previous studies (Boesel and Johnson, 1988; Garcia and Joy, 1998; and Garcia et al., 2002) that show TA users are more likely to stay in the military than are nonusers. We show that these studies did not adequately control for the length of time that stayers and leavers were eligible to use TA. Leavers are in the military for substantially less time and inherently less likely to use TA than were similar stayers because they are eligible for fewer months. The authors of the earlier studies incorrectly infer that TA users are more likely to stay than nonusers, but the data are simply showing that stayers have more opportunity to use TA. We reestimated these models and showed that TA users were consistently less likely to remain in the military than nonusers, when both groups were eligible for TA for equal periods of time.

The results from our two models and the reestimation of the previous models suggest that marines and sailors are using TA programs to prepare for postservice education or jobs. Two factors are likely to contribute to this outcome. First, the GI Bill provides benefits to cover college expenses after military service. Second, deployments and work conflicts make it difficult for members to accumulate college credits and progress toward a degree. Members anxious to earn a degree may see little reason to pursue their studies as a full-time marine or sailor. Rather, they can leave the military and attend school (either full- or part-time) under their GI Bill benefits.

TA may have important recruiting benefits that help recoup the cost of the program. Most new recruits are interested in pursuing further education, and 62 percent of recruits claimed that education benefits and opportunities were a primary reason why they joined the military (1999 Active-Duty Survey). We have seen no formal estimates of what share of recruits joined specifically because of TA opportunities. In our focus group discussions with members, they were enthusiastic about TA and saw the program as an important benefit, but many were frustrated that their work schedule limited their opportunities to enroll in college classes.

In addition, DoD and Congress have a long-standing commitment to enhance the education of military members. Postservice education benefits along with TA have been available for more than 50 years. These programs have been predicated, at least in part, in rewarding members for their military service.

REESTIMATION OF THE BOESEL AND JOHNSON RETENTION MODEL

This appendix shows that the results of Boesel and Johnson (1988) are sensitive to the modeling approach used in their study. They compare the retention rates of Tuition Assistance (TA) users and nonusers over an 18-month window from July 1986 through December 1987. They find that the retention rates of TA users are 11 percentage points higher than for comparable members who did not participate in TA.

This result is misleading, because retained and separated members have different opportunities to use the TA program. Retained members have the option of using TA anytime during the 18-month window, but members who leave during the 18 months lose the option of participating in TA. If losses were equally spaced over the 18-month interval, then the typical leaver would have only nine months to use TA as compared with 18 months for all stayers. Suppose, for example, that retention and TA usage *in each month* were completely unrelated. The TA usage rate of a member who left midway through the 18 months would then be lower that of a member who completed the full 18 months in the military. Then, the stayers would have higher TA usage than the leavers over the 18-month window, but this would simply reflect differences in the number of months that stayers and leavers were eligible for TA. The modeling approach of Boesel and Johnson exaggerates the tendency of TA users to have higher retention than nonusers.

We considered an alternative modeling approach that looks at member retention in one period as a function of TA participation in a previous period. This approach mirrors Boesel and Johnson's model, but it looks at whether TA participation in one 18-month period is a predictor of retention in the following 18-month period. We only consider members who are in the military for the entire 18-month initial window, so subsequent stayers and leavers all have equal access to TA.

We estimated separate results for the Marine Corps and Navy.[1] The sample is based on marines and sailors who were in the military in October 1994. Our first model duplicates the Boesel and Johnson (1988) approach for the 18-month window from October 1994 through March 1996. The approach examines how TA usage during these months affects retention over the same period, while controlling for a variety of demographic variables as well as military tenure and pay grade.[2] The second model considers retention in the next 18-month period (April 1996 through September) as a function of TA usage in the initial period and the same control variables. We want to compare whether the effect of TA usage on retention is more positive in the first model than in the second, because members who left before March 1996 had less opportunity to use TA than those who remained in the military through March 1996.

Table A.1 shows the results for the Marine Corps. Our results for the first model show that TA users have retention rates 5 percentage points higher than nonusers during the initial 18-month window. This finding is consistent with the Boesel and Johnson (1988) result that TA users have higher retention than nonusers. We think that this result is a by-product of a flawed methodology, however. The results from the second model show that the retention rate of TA users in the next 18-month period is 12 percentage points lower than for TA nonusers.

---

[1] The Navy is more than twice the size of the Marine Corps. For efficiency reasons, we based our analysis on a twenty percent random sample of sailors. We used the entire Marine Corps dataset in our analysis.

[2] As discussed in Chapter Two, we do not believe that attrition and reenlistment should be combined. In addition, the effects of TA usage and other variables on retention may vary with time in the military and pay grade. Boesel and Johnson (1988) include military tenure and pay grade as control variables, but these variables reflect member choices and may bias the parameter estimates. For comparison purposes, we have duplicated their specification in this appendix.

Table A.1

Marine Corps Results

Variable	Retention (October 1994–March 1996)		Retention (April 1996–September 1997)	
	Coefficient	Standard Error	Coefficient	Standard Error
TA Usage (October 1994–March 1995)	0.0540*	0.0041	−0.1199*	0.0055
Female	−0.0313*	0.0061	0.0464*	0.0071
Black	0.0497*	0.0030	0.0798*	0.0038
Hispanic	0.0439*	0.0038	0.0404*	0.0048
Asian/Pacific Islander	0.0498*	0.0082	0.0774*	0.0100
Category 1 (AFQT 93–99 Percentile)	−0.2480*	0.0147	−0.0958*	0.0140
Category 2 (AFQT 65–92 Percentile)	−0.2395*	0.0112	−0.0981*	0.0112
Category 3a (AFQT 50–64 Percentile)	−0.2503*	0.0118	−0.1210*	0.0115
Category 3b (AFQT 31–49 Percentile)	−0.2399*	0.0116	−0.1256*	0.0114
Non–High School Graduate	−0.1357*	0.0322	−0.0612	0.0445
GED	0.0281*	0.0078	−0.0205	0.0108
Alternative Education Credential	0.0070	0.0069	0.0201*	0.0089
Some College	−0.0187*	0.0074	−0.0087	0.0092
Single Parent	0.0061	0.0058	0.0287*	0.0072
Married	−0.0015	0.0027	0.0463*	0.0034
Joint Military Couple	0.0381*	0.0073	0.0025	0.0097
Months in Military	−0.0024*	0.0000	−0.0007*	0.0001
Pay Grade	0.1245*	0.0017	0.0890*	0.0025
Proportion Retained	0.7475		0.6615	
Sample Size	147,970		110,604	

NOTE: The estimated effects (dF/dX) correspond to changes in the probability relative to the excluded reference category for discrete variables and the derivative of the probability for continuous variables. Entries with asterisks are associated with coefficients significant at the $\alpha = 0.05$ confidence level.

The reference categories for demographic variables in the model are male, white non-Hispanic, high school diploma graduate, and single with no children.

The Navy results in Table A.2 are similar to those for the Marine Corps. The result from the Boesel and Johnson model shows that Navy retention is 3 percentage points higher for TA users than for nonusers when usage and retention are measured over the same 18-

Table A.2

Navy Results

Variable	Retention (October 1994–March 1996)		Retention (April 1996–September 1997)	
	Coefficient	Standard Error	Coefficient	Standard Error
TA Usage (October 1994–March 1995)	0.0327*	0.0057	−0.0829*	0.0073
Female	−0.0074	0.0050	−0.0001	0.0058
Black	0.0453*	0.0040	0.0643*	0.0045
Hispanic	0.0097	0.0058	0.0193*	0.0066
Asian/Pacific Islander	0.0831*	0.0060	0.1056*	0.0065
Category 1 (AFQT 93–99 Percentile)	−0.1534*	0.0128	−0.0640*	0.0127
Category 2 (AFQT 65–92 Percentile)	−0.1188*	0.0087	−0.0548*	0.0093
Category 3a (AFQT 50–64 Percentile)	−0.1091*	0.0094	−0.0405*	0.0097
Category 3b AFQT 31–49 Percentile)	−0.0839*	0.0087	−0.0364*	0.0091
Non–High School Graduate	0.0042	0.0097	0.0149	0.0116
GED	0.0046	0.0084	0.0227*	0.0098
Alternative Education Credential	0.0058	0.0171	−0.0693*	0.0223
Some College	−0.0045	0.0080	0.0054	0.0089
Single Parent	0.0122	0.0063	0.0296*	0.0071
Married	0.0382*	0.0038	0.0734*	0.0045
Joint Military Couple	0.0309*	0.0086	0.0108	0.0100
Months in Military	−0.0023*	0.0000	−0.0011*	0.0001
Pay Grade	0.1196*	0.0019	0.0959*	0.0025
Proportion Retained	0.7671		0.7452	
Sample Size	79,980		61,275	

NOTE: The estimated effects (dF/dX) correspond to changes in the probability relative to the excluded reference category for discrete variables and the derivative of the probability for continuous variables. Entries with asterisks are associated with coefficients significant at the $\alpha = 0.05$ confidence level.

The reference categories for demographic variables in the model are male, white non-Hispanic, high school diploma graduate, and single with no children.

month window. This finding is misleading, however, because leaving members had less opportunity to use TA than stayers. The second model shows that TA users had retention rates 8 percentage points lower than nonusers, when usage is measured over an equal-length window prior to the retention decision.

The empirical results confirm our suspicion that the Boesel and Johnson (1988) result is driven by the fact that members who leave the military during the 18-month window have less opportunity to use TA than do members who stay 18 months. When looking at TA usage over a constant time interval, we see that TA usage is actually lower for members who stay than for members that leave.

REESTIMATION OF THE GARCIA AND JOY (1998) CONTINUATION MODEL

Garcia and Joy (1998) built a model to examine who stays in the Navy beyond the end of their four-year enlistment term. They compared the attributes of sailors who leave *on or before* the end of their term with those of sailors who reenlist at the end of their term or extend their term for at least one year. This approach may create problems because the leavers are a heterogeneous population group. About one-third of each entry cohort leaves without completing the end of their initial term. Many of these sailors are unproductive or unsuitable for the Navy and are encouraged to leave. In contrast, members who successfully complete their term and then leave are better matched with the Navy, and most would be allowed to stay if they choose to do so. For these reasons, most military personnel studies separate the analysis of first-term attrition (i.e., who does and does not complete their term successfully) from first-term reenlistment (i.e., who among the first-term completers stays beyond the first term). For example, Warner and Solon (1991) estimate separate models of first-term attrition and reenlistment. They show that many demographic factors have a different effect on attrition than on reenlistment.

The measure of continuation rates is particularly ill-suited to identifying whether TA usage encourages sailors to stay in the Navy. The typical early leaver in the FY 1992 cohort had only 1.8 years in the Navy, compared with the four years of members who complete their term. These early leavers have much less opportunity to use TA by virtue of 2.2 fewer years of eligibility. The continuation of TA users is prone to be higher than that of nonusers because these early leavers have only a short eligibility for TA, compared with members who complete their term.

Table B.1 shows our estimates of factors affecting the continuation rate. These results parallel those of Garcia and Joy (1998): TA users are estimated to have continuation rates 5 percentage points lower than those of nonusers.[1] Table B.1 also shows estimates of a traditional reenlistment equation where early leavers (i.e., attrition) are deleted from the sample. In this case, all sailors complete four years of service, so the TA eligibility is held constant at four years. The results show that reenlistment rates are 6 percentage points lower for TA users than for nonusers. The results in Table B.1 suggest that the positive effect of TA usage on continuation in the Garcia and Joy (1998) study is driven by the limited access to TA for early leavers. When members have an equal-length period to use TA, TA users are more likely to leave the Navy than are nonusers.

Table B.1

Probit Regression Results for Effect of TA Usage of Continuation and Reenlistment Rates of Four-Year Sailors in the FY 1992 Cohort

Variable	Continuation Rate		Reenlistment Rate	
	Coefficient	Standard Error	Coefficient	Standard Error
TA User	0.0502*	0.0209	−0.0590*	0.0276
Female	0.0374*	0.0182	0.0403	0.0266
Age at Entry	0.0056*	0.0026	0.0126*	0.0036
Black	0.1295*	0.0170	0.1751*	0.0239
Hispanic	0.0517*	0.0198	0.0840*	0.0276
Asian/Pacific Islander	0.1318*	0.0340	0.1559*	0.0461
AFQT Score	0.0134	0.0075	0.0089	0.0103
GED or No Degree	0.0846	0.0700	0.2097	0.1092
Some College	0.0376	0.0505	−0.0396	0.0675
Single Parent	0.0504	0.0259	0.0397	0.0363
Married	0.1786*	0.0129	0.1629*	0.0177
Percentage of Time at Sea	−0.2916*	0.0711	−0.4306*	0.0995
Percentage of Time at Sea Squared	0.5885*	0.0727	0.5705*	0.0990

---

[1]The estimates presented here are simpler than the two-equation model estimated by Garcia and Joy (1998). We are focusing on the sensitivity of the TA effect to the definition of continuation and reenlistment.

Electronic Equipment Repair	0.0299	0.0271	0.0433	0.0366
Communications/Intelligence	0.0751*	0.0287	0.0492	0.0377
Health Care	0.2304*	0.0290	0.1992*	0.0392
Other Technical and Allied	0.2455*	0.0668	0.2652*	0.0914
Functional Support and Administrative	0.1061*	0.0285	0.1573*	0.0391
Electrical/Mechanical Equipment Repair	0.0078	0.0236	−0.0113	0.0314
Craftsman	−0.1767*	0.0404	−0.2113*	0.0533
Service and Supply Handler	−0.0249	0.0306	0.0197	0.0421
Not Occupationally Qualified	−0.0613*	0.0228	0.0098	0.0316
Constant	−0.6291*	0.0734	−0.5715*	0.1031
Proportion Staying	0.2809		0.4214	
Sample Size	5,383		3,588	

NOTE: The estimated effects (dF/dX) correspond to changes in the probability relative to the excluded reference category for discrete variables and the derivative of the probability for continuous variables. Entries with asterisks are associated with coefficients significant at the $\alpha = 0.05$ confidence level.

Continuation compares members who extend their enlistment for one year or reenlist with members who leave on *or before* the end of their term. Reenlistment deletes from the continuation sample members who leave before the end of their term—i.e., it focuses on the stay-or-leave decision of members who complete their term.

The reference categories for demographic variables in the model are male, white non-Hispanic, high school diploma graduate, single with no children, and assigned to an occupational group of infantry, gun crews, and seamanship specialists.

REESTIMATION OF THE GARCIA et al.
CONTINUATION MODEL

Garcia et al. (2002) show that the average TA user has a 72-month completion rate that is 11 to 13 percentage points higher than the average sailor who does not use TA. Their results are based on an analysis of the retention and tuition usage patterns of a cohort of sailors that enlisted in FY 1992 and were tracked for six years.[1] Garcia et al. (2002) infer that members stay longer because of the availability of TA.

We believe that this study suffers from the same problem as the Boesel and Johnson (1988) study—i.e., the authors consider retention and TA usage over a fixed-length window and do not account for the leavers having much less opportunity to use TA than stayers. Military losses are bunched at low years of service as unsuitable sailors are weeded out and dissatisfied sailors complete their initial enlistments and leave the Navy. For the 1992 cohort, 21 percent of sailors completing six years used TA as compared with only 8 percent of sailors who left before completing six years. Leavers had substantially less opportunity to use TA, however, because the typical leaver was only in the Navy for 2.3 years, compared with the six years of TA eligibility for stayers. In large part, stayers are more likely to use TA than leavers because they have many more months of eligibility for the program. Even if stayers and leavers were equally likely to use TA in a given month, we would still observe that members remaining six

---

[1]The authors restricted their sample to Navy recruits who were initially obligated to a two-, three-, or four-year term in the Navy. Our sample also uses this restriction.

years would have a much higher usage rate than members remaining 2.3 years. The Garcia et al. (2002) approach confounds the effect of TA usage on retention with the fact that retained members have much more opportunity to use TA.

A more reasonable comparison would be to look at sailors who completed a fixed interval of time (say, five years) and see whether TA users during that interval have a higher retention rate in the next year than do TA nonusers over the same interval. This approach automatically fixes time that members are eligible for TA and looks forward to see whether TA usage affects subsequent retention.

We used our Navy data from the 1992 cohort to reestimate the Garcia et al. (2002) model of six-year continuation. The results in the first column of Table C.1 shows that TA users have completion rates 14 percentage points higher than do TA nonusers.[2] This TA "effect" corresponds to the finding of the earlier study. Sailors who leave are only eligible for TA before separation, so the window of opportunity for TA usage differs for leavers and stayers.

The next several columns of the table show the results of one-year retention conditional on a fixed-length window of TA availability. For example, the second column shows whether TA usage over the first five years in the Navy predicts retention in the sixth year. By construction, the model in the second column only includes members who complete five years in the Navy because others would not have had a five-year opportunity to use TA. The results show that sailors who used TA during their first five years in the Navy have sixth-year retention rates that are 9 percentage points *lower* than those of TA nonusers over the same five-year window. This suggests that TA usage has a negative effect on retention, perhaps because TA users leave for full-time college or to use their training in civilian jobs.

The remaining regression specifications in Table C.1 show one-year retention for sailors with differing length windows of opportunity for using TA. The results from each specification show that TA usage

---

[2]The regression specification includes demographic and occupational controls similar to those of the earlier study.

over a fixed interval is always associated with reduced retention in the subsequent period.

The empirical results in Table C.1 show that the positive effect of TA usage on retention in Garcia et al. (2002) is misleading, because stayers and leavers do not have equal access to the TA program. When TA usage is measured over a fixed interval, TA users are consistently less likely to remain in the Navy than are nonusers.

Table C.1

Probit Regression Results for Effects of TA Usage on Navy Retention

Dependent Variable	Stay Six Years	Equal Time Eligible for TA			
		Stay Sixth Year	Stay Fifth Year	Stay Fourth Year	Stay Third Year
Years Eligible for TA	Variable	5	4	3	2
Characteristic					
TA User	0.1355*	−0.0936*	−0.0628*	−0.0512*	−0.0637*
Female	−0.0407*	−0.0361	−0.0094	−0.0134	−0.0113
Age at Entry	0.0066*	−0.0001	0.0152*	0.0018	0.0057*
Black	0.1153*	0.0649*	0.1561*	0.0450*	0.0687*
Hispanic	0.0437*	0.0079	0.0749*	−0.0007	0.0293
Asian/Pacific Islander	0.1306*	0.0505	0.1820*	0.0656	0.1237*
AFQT Score	−0.0043	−0.0106	0.0033	0.0078	0.0044
GED or No Degree	0.0421	0.1595	0.0685	−0.0196	0.0563
Some College	−0.0108	0.0642	−0.0563	0.0379	−0.0533
Single Parent	0.0407	−0.0007	0.0887	−0.0012	0.0423
Married	0.0452*	0.0058	0.0807*	0.0197	0.0303
Electronic Equipment Repair	−0.0102	0.0125	0.0099	−0.0460	−0.0166
Communications/Intelligence	0.0334	0.0193	0.0087	−0.0254	0.0975*
Health Care	0.0725*	0.0069	0.1122*	0.0611*	0.0678*
Other Technical and Allied	0.1241*	0.0451	0.1836	0.0099	0.2624
Functional Support and Administrative	0.0401	0.0138	0.1231*	0.0050	0.0009
Electrical/Mechanical Equipment Repair	−0.0188	−0.0246	−0.0659*	−0.0117	0.0200
Craftsman	−0.1086*	−0.0807	−0.1882*	−0.0678*	−0.0016

Table C.1—Continued

Dependent Variable	Stay Six Years	Equal Time Eligible for TA			
		Stay Sixth Year	Stay Fifth Year	Stay Fourth Year	Stay Third Year
Years Eligible for TA	Variable	5	4	3	2
Service and Supply Handler	−0.0330	−0.0389	−0.0381	0.0093	−0.0424
Not Occupationally Qualified	−0.0857*	0.0004	−0.0134	0.0137	−0.0750*
Two- or Three-Year Term	−0.1078*	0.0135	0.4116*	0.1298*	−0.5014*
Constant	−0.3271*	0.2994*	−0.3642*	0.1358	0.1961*
Proportion Staying	0.2115	0.8714	0.4537	0.7975	0.7336
Sample Size	7,819	1,898	3,491	4,377	5,942

NOTE: The estimated effects (dF/dX) correspond to changes in the probability relative to the excluded reference category for discrete variables and the derivative of the probability for continuous variables. Entries with asterisks are associated with coefficients significant at the $\alpha = 0.05$ confidence level.

The reference categories for demographic variables in the model are male, white non-Hispanic, high school diploma graduate, and single with no children. The reference groups for military characteristics are infantry, gun crews, and seamanship specialists and four-year enlistment term.

A BIVARIATE PROBIT MODEL OF TA USAGE
AND REENLISTMENT

INTRODUCTION

This report develops a model of the impact of TA on reenlistment. Reenlistment depends on the demographic characteristics of the individual as well as the nature of his or her occupation and military experiences (e.g., sea duty or deployment). In addition, reenlistment may depend on whether or not an individual takes college courses while in the military. The military services pay the costs of these courses under the TA program as an employee benefit to military members. We treat participation in TA as an endogenous variable in this model because individuals with higher ability (unmeasured by the analyst) may be more likely to take TA courses. Unmeasured individual ability may also have a direct impact on reenlistment. Therefore, the estimate of the effect of TA on reenlistment in a model that does not account for the endogeneity of TA may be biased. To address the potential endogeneity of TA, we estimate a bivariate probit model of TA participation and reenlistment.

The tendency to take a TA course is the second equation in the bivariate probit model. TA usage depends on a set of factors similar to those for reenlistment. In addition, TA usage may depend on the TA opportunities available at the individual's base and the member's underlying "taste" for college classes. While TA opportunities available at the individual's base should be expected to affect the individual's tendency to take TA courses, these opportunities should have no direct effect on individual reenlistment. Members who grew up near four-year colleges are expected to have more interest in college than others. Proximity to college should have a direct effect on TA usage, but we don't expect this variable to have a direct effect on retention. Therefore, TA opportunities and proximity to a four-year college at accession are included as explanatory variables in the TA equation, but excluded from the reenlistment equation. This bivariate probit model is an extension of the "instrumental variable" approach to the case where both outcome variables (reenlistment and TA participation) are dichotomous variables. The mathematical model below formalizes these notions and prepares for an empirical analysis of reenlistment and TA.

THE MODEL

The tendency to reenlist is uncertain (to the analyst) because not all factors affecting reenlistment can be measured. The tendency to reenlist is a continuous random variable but is only observed as a dichotomous variable that indicates whether or not an individual reenlists. In other words, the tendency to reenlist is a latent (i.e., not directly observed) random variable. The individual's tendency to reenlist, denoted by R_i^*, is modeled as a function of a (column) vector of observed variables, X_i a (row) vector of unobserved parameters β_1, an indicator variable that denotes whether or not the individual took a TA course, TA_i and its corresponding parameter γ, and an unobserved random error ε_{1i}. The subscript i denotes an individual.

$$R_i^* = \beta_1 X_i + \gamma TA_i + \varepsilon_{1i}$$

The explanatory variables in X_i include such servicemember demographic characteristics as age, sex, race, marital status, education, and AFQT score categories. X_i also includes variables on the servicemembers' occupation and months deployed during the year. The variable R_i^* is a continuous measure of the tendency to reenlist. In fact, the investigator only observes the action to reenlist, so the observed variable, R_i, is truncated as a zero-one variable:

$$R_i = \begin{cases} 1 \text{ if } R_i^* > 0 \\ 0 \text{ otherwise} \end{cases}$$

To determine which factors influence servicemembers' tendency to take TA courses, we develop an equation for the tendency to take a TA course as part of the bivariate probit model. As with the tendency to reenlist, the tendency to take a TA course is an unobserved latent variable. The individual's tendency to take a TA course, denoted by TA_i^*, is modeled as a function of a (column) vector of observed variables, X_i, a (row) vector of unobserved parameters β_2, a set of variables that measures the TA opportunities available on the individual's base, Z_i their corresponding parameters δ, and an unobserved random error ε_{2i}. Z_i is excluded from the reenlistment equation presented earlier. The subscript i denotes an individual.

$$TA_i^* = \beta_2 X_i + \delta Z_i + \varepsilon_{2i}$$

The explanatory variables in X_i include the same set of variables as described earlier. The variable TA_i^* is a continuous measure of the tendency to take a TA course, but the investigator observes only whether or not a course is taken, so the observed variable, TA_i^*, is truncated as a zero-one variable:

$$TA_i = \begin{cases} 1 \text{ if } TA_i^* > 0 \\ 0 \text{ otherwise} \end{cases}$$

This set of equations constitutes the model of TA usage and reenlistment. The model is capable of explaining the set of four possible qualitative outcomes regarding TA and reenlistment, once stochastic assumptions are made.

STOCHASTIC ASSUMPTIONS AND ESTIMATION

Assume that ε_1 and ε_2 are jointly bivariate normal with zero means and variance covariance matrix:

$$\Sigma = \begin{bmatrix} \sigma_{11} & \sigma_{12} \\ \sigma_{12} & \sigma_{22} \end{bmatrix}$$

That is, $V(\varepsilon_1) = \sigma_{11} = 1$, $V(\varepsilon_2) = \sigma_{22} = 1$, and $Cov(\varepsilon_1, \varepsilon_2) = \sigma_{12} = \rho$. Notice that the variance of ε_1 and ε_2 are normalized to one since the scale of R_i and TA_i are not observed. As a result, $\sigma_{12} = \rho$.

We can estimate the two-equation system under these stochastic assumptions using a bivariate probit maximum likelihood model. The likelihood function is given by:

$$L = \sum_{i=1}^{n} \ln \Phi_2(q_{1i}\xi_{1i}, q_{2i}\xi_{2i}, \rho_i^*)$$

where

$$q_{1i} = 2R_i - 1,$$

therefore, for a reenlister $q_{1i} = 1$, and for a separator $q_{1i} = -1$,

$$q_{2i} = 2TA_i - 1$$

and similarly for a course taker, $q_{2i} = 1$, and for a nontaker $q_{2i} = -1$, and

$$\xi_{1i} = \beta_1 X_i + \gamma TA_i,$$

from the reenlistment equation,

$$\xi_{2i} = \beta_2 X_i + \delta Z_i,$$

from the TA equation, and

$$\rho_i^* = q_{1i}q_{2i}\rho.$$

Note that Φ_2 is used to denote the cumulative density function of the bivariate normal density.

The model can be summarized by four regimes depending on whether the individual takes a TA course or not and whether the individual reenlists or not. Table D.1 shows how these regimes depend on model parameters and gives the underlying probability of each regime occurring.

Table D.1.

Summary of Model Regimes

Regime	Event in Terms of ε_1 and ε_2	Probability
Reenlistment and TA	$\varepsilon_{1i} < \xi_{1i}, \varepsilon_{2i} < \xi_{2i}$	$\Phi_2(\xi_{1i}, \xi_{2i}, \rho)$
Separation and TA	$\varepsilon_{1i} < -\xi_{1i}, \varepsilon_{2i} < \xi_{2i}$	$\Phi_2(-\xi_{1i}, \xi_{2i}, -\rho)$
Reenlistment and no TA	$\varepsilon_{1i} < \xi_{1i}, \varepsilon_{2i} < -\xi_{2i}$	$\Phi_2(\xi_{1i}, -\xi_{2i}, -\rho)$
Separation and no TA	$\varepsilon_{1i} < -\xi_{1i}, \varepsilon_{2i} < -\xi_{2i}$	$\Phi_2(-\xi_{1i}, -\xi_{2i}, \rho)$

These probabilities show that, for example, the contribution to the likelihood function for an individual who reenlists and takes TA courses is:

$$Pr(\varepsilon_{1i} < \xi_{1i}, \varepsilon_{2i} < \xi_{2i}) = \phi_2(\xi_{1i}, \xi_{2i}, \rho)$$

Maximization of this bivariate probit maximum likelihood function yields consistent, asymptotically efficient estimates of the model coefficients and the covariance matrix. The correlation between the errors in the two equations, ρ, can be interpreted as the interdependence of the unobserved components in the TA and the reenlistment equations.

Because of the nonlinear nature of the bivariate probit maximum likelihood model, interpretation of the coefficients is not as straightforward as with linear models. For the continuous variables, such as age and months deployed, we calculate partial derivatives to aid interpretation. The partial derivatives can be interpreted as the effect of a one-unit increase in the X variable on the outcome variable being considered. For binary variables, such as TA in the reenlistment equation, we use the model coefficients to predict the average rate of reenlistment in the sample after TA is set to one for the full sample. Next, we predict the average rate of reenlistment in the sample when TA is set to zero for the full sample. The difference between these two rates of reenlistment is interpreted as the effect of TA on reenlistment.

Anderson, Clinton L., and Steve F. Kline, *Adult Higher Education and the Military: Blending Traditional and Nontraditional Education,* Washington, D.C.: American Association of State Colleges and Universities, 1990.

Anderson, Clinton L., "The Tuition Assistance Program in the Military," Report to U.S. Army Forces Command, Lexington, Ky., 1991.

Angrist, Joshua D., "Conditional Independence in Sample Selection Models," *Economic Letters,* Vol. 54, 1997, pp. 103–112.

_____, "Estimation of Limited Dependent Variable Models with Dummy Endogenous Regressors: Simple Strategies for Empirical Practice," *Journal of Business and Economic Statistics,* Vol. 19, No. 1, 1999, pp. 2–28.

Barnard, John, Constantine Frangakis, Jennifer Hill, and Donald B. Rubin, "School Choice in NY City: A Bayesian Analysis of an Imperfect Randomized Experiment," in C. Gatsonis et al., eds., *Case Studies in Bayesian Statistics,* New York: Springer-Verlag, 2001.

Boesel, David, and Kyle Johnson, *The DoD Tuition Assistance Program: Participation and Outcomes,* Arlington, Virginia: Defense Manpower Data Center, May 1988.

Buddin, Richard, *Promotion Tempo and Enlisted Retention,* Santa Monica, Calif.: RAND, R-4135-FMP, 1992.

_____, *Building a Personnel Support Agenda: Goals, Analysis Framework, and Data Requirements,* Santa Monica, Calif.: RAND, MR-916, 1998.

_____, Carole Roan Gresenz, Susan D. Hosek, Marc N. Elliott, and Jennifer Hawes-Dawson, *An Evaluation of Housing Options for Military Families,* Santa Monica, Calif.: RAND, MR-1020, 1999.

Card, David, "Using Geographic Variation in College Proximity to Estimate the Return to Schooling," Cambridge, Mass.: National Bureau of Economic Research, Working Paper No. 4483, October 1993.

Dehejia, Rajeev H., and Sadek Wahba, "Causal Effects in Nonexperimental Studies: Reevaluating the Evaluation of Training Programs," *Journal of the American Statistical Association,* Vol. 94, No. 448, December 1999.

Garcia, Federico E., Jeremy Arkes, and Robert Trost, "Does Employer-Financed General Training Pay? Evidence from the U.S. Navy," *Economics of Education Review,* Vol. 21, 2002.

_____, and Ernest H. Joy with David L. Reese, *Effectiveness of the Voluntary Education Program,* Alexandria, Va.: Center for Naval Analyses, CRM-98-40, April 1998.

Heckman, James J., Hidehiko Ichimura, and Petra E. Todd, "Matching as an Econometric Evaluation Estimator: Evidence from Evaluating a Job Training Programme," *Review of Economic Studies,* Vol. 64, No. 4, 1997, pp. 605–654.

Hirano, Keisuke, Guido W. Imbens, and Geert Ridder, "Efficient Estimation of Average Treatment Effects Using the Estimated Propensity Score," Technical Working Paper 251, National Bureau of Economic Research, March 2000.

Hosek, James, and Mark Totten, *Does Perstempo Hurt Reenlistment? The Effect of Long or Hostile Perstempo on Reenlistment,* Santa Monica, Calif.: RAND, MR-990-OSD, 1998.

Ichimura, Hidehiko, and Christopher Taber, "Propensity-Score Matching with Instrumental Variables," *American Economic Review,* Vol. 91, No. 2, 2001, pp. 119–124.

Kane, Thomas J., and Cecelia Elena Rouse, "Labor-Market Returns to Two- and Four-Year College," *American Economic Review,* June 1995, pp. 600–614.

_____, and Cecilia Elena Rouse, "The Community College: Educating Students at the Margin Between College and Work," *Journal of Economic Perspectives,* Vol. 13, No. 1, Winter 1999, pp. 63–84.

Leigh, Duane E., and Andrew M. Gill, "Labor Market Returns to Community Colleges: Evidence for Returning Adults," *Journal of Human Resources,* Vol. 32, No. 2, Spring 1997.

Rosenbaum, Paul R., and Donald B. Rubin, "Constructing a Control Group Using Multivariate Matched Sampling Methods That Incorporate the Propensity Score," *American Statistician,* Vol. 39, No. 1, February 1985.

Rouse, Cecilia Elena, "What to Do After High School: The Two-Year Versus Four-Year College Enrollment Decision," in Ronald Ehrenberg, ed., *Choices and Consequences: Contemporary Issues in Education Policy,* New York: ILR Press, 1994, pp. 59–88.

Tiemeyer, Peter, Casey Wardynski, and Richard Buddin, *Financial Management Problems Among Enlisted Personnel,* Santa Monica, Calif.: RAND, DB-241-OSD, 1999.

Warner, John, and Gary Solon, "First-Term Attrition and Reenlistment in the U.S. Army," in Curtis L. Gilroy, David K. Horne, and D. Alton Smith, eds., *Military Compensation and Personnel Retention: Models and Evidence,* Alexandria, Va.: U.S. Army Research Institute for the Behavioral and Social Sciences, 1991, pp. 243–277.